MARKETING WITHOUT A MARKETING BUDGET

MARKETING WITHOUT A MARKETING BUDGET

How to find customers yesterday, on a shoestring, without fouling up your schedule any worse than it already is…

Craig S. Rice
Former President,
Royal Crown Cola, Ltd., Canada

BOB ADAMS, INC.
PUBLISHERS

Copyright © 1989 Craig Rice. All rights reserved. No part of this work may be reproduced in any form without permission of the publisher.

Cover illustration by Jim M'Guinness.

ISBN: 1-55850-986-0

Published by Bob Adams, Inc., 260 Center Street, Holbrook MA 02343.

Printed in the United States of America.

Dedication

This book is dedicated to the many proprietors and managers in small- and medium-sized businesses who face new marketing challenges, problems, and opportunities every day.

Acknowledgments

Thanks are due to the efforts of many people who contributed to this book, including:

My colleagues and fellow instructors at the University of Chicago, De Paul University, Northwestern University, Burnett, Armour, Procter & Gamble, Royal Crown, ConAgra, and SBA.

My good wife Gwen and our four grown children, Kathy, Carol, Doug, and Steve, who provided their indispensable patience, love, encouragement, suggestions, and support.

Last, but not least, Brandon Toropov at Bob Adams, Inc., for his work in editing and developing the manuscript.

"Our first duty is not to be poor."

George Bernard Shaw

Table of Contents

PREFACE/19

"Why are so many marketing books user-hostile?" 21

WHY DO I NEED MARKETING?/25

"What is marketing?" 27
"Is marketing really necessary?" 31
"Marketing can sell anything . . . can't it?" 35

FIRST STEPS/37

"Why is quality important--and how do I know when I'm delivering it?" 39
"What's my first step?" 43
"If I'm just a small business, do I still need a plan?" 47
"Why should I do so much preparation?" 51
"How do market facts help me come out on top?" 53
"What if I'm wrong?" 55

LOTS OF CHEAP IDEAS THAT CAN INCREASE SALES IN A HURRY/57

"How can I generate more sales if I don't have much money to spend--or none at all?" 59

"What promotions can I use to make business really take off?" 69

"How can I increase referrals from customers?" 71

"Why is packaging important?" 73

"What about packaging a service, rather than a product?" 75

"How can I use free samples to build my sales?" 77

"What are shelftalkers?" 81

"How can I get free publicity from the media?" 85

"I got a booking on an interview show! Now what?" 91

"How can I take advantage of trade publications and industry newsletters?" 93

"Can I build sales with only a ream of letter-sized paper and some three-by-five cards?" 97

"How can I target the first-time customer--and get the person to come back for more?" 103

"I'm putting together a catalog on the cheap--how do I make sure it delivers results?" 107

"We don't use catalogs--our emphasis is on handbills and flyers. Something that simple is hard to mess up, isn't it?" 111

"Is it worth my while to consider using direct-mail marketing?" 115

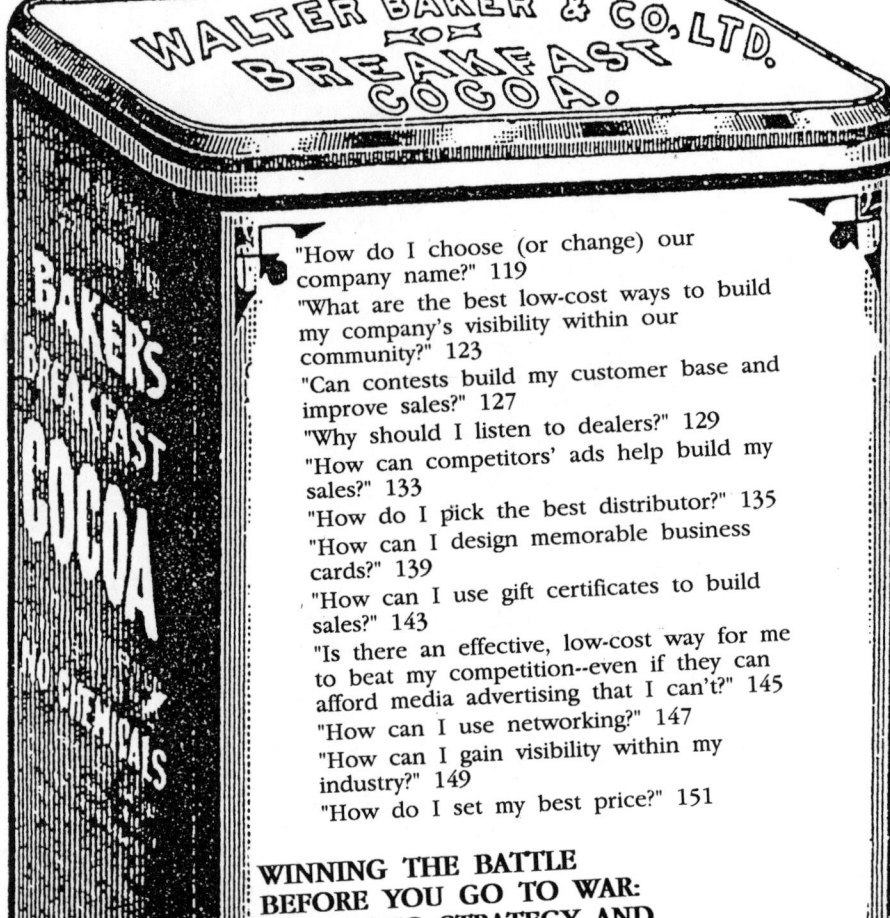

"How do I choose (or change) our company name?" 119
"What are the best low-cost ways to build my company's visibility within our community?" 123
"Can contests build my customer base and improve sales?" 127
"Why should I listen to dealers?" 129
"How can competitors' ads help build my sales?" 133
"How do I pick the best distributor?" 135
"How can I design memorable business cards?" 139
"How can I use gift certificates to build sales?" 143
"Is there an effective, low-cost way for me to beat my competition--even if they can afford media advertising that I can't?" 145
"How can I use networking?" 147
"How can I gain visibility within my industry?" 149
"How do I set my best price?" 151

WINNING THE BATTLE BEFORE YOU GO TO WAR: MARKETING STRATEGY AND TACTICS FOR YOUR BUSINESS/155

"My competition is killing me! What do I do?" 157
"How do I market in tough business conditions?" 161

"We're doing great! Any suggestions on how best to market during the good times?" 165
"What about putting together the budget?" 167
"Can a small company like mine implement successful marketing and management ideas from the Japanese?" 175
"What about Japanese 'quality circles'? How can they help our marketing efforts?" 179

PERSON-TO-PERSON: IDEAS OF SPECIAL INTEREST TO RETAILERS, RESTAURANT OPERATORS, AND OTHER "PEOPLE" FIELDS/181

"I run a small retail operation. How can I win customers from the big guys?" 183
"If I'm in retail, I don't have to worry about packaging, do I?" 187
"Will I sell more if my inventory is large and varied?" 189
"How can I run the most effective low-cost marketing campaign for my restaurant?" 193
"I'm going to be concentrating on developing a home-based business. What's the best marketing approach for me?" 197
"Is it absolutely necessary to advertise in the Yellow Pages?" 201

TO ADVERTISE OR NOT TO ADVERTISE/205

"Should I advertise?" 207
"If I decide to advertise, how can I pick cost-effective media that will do the job?" 209
"How do I put the ad together?" 213
"How do the big corporations decide if an ad's worth spending money on?" 217

"I'm uncomfortable developing ad copy. Should I consider using an ad agency?" 227
"Broadly speaking, which medium is more cost-effective--television or radio?" 231

PERSONAL SELLING FOR SUCCESS (OR: POOR SALESPEOPLE HAVE SKINNY KIDS!)/235

"I'm going to be doing a lot of our company's in-person selling work. Any suggestions?" 237
"Does management by objective work in personal sales settings?" 241
"How do I put together my pitch?" 245
"How do I sell by phone?" 251
"What are the best ways to build up repeat business in my personal sales work?" 255
"How do I hire really good salespeople?" 257
"How much should I pay my salespeople?" 261
"How do I keep salespeople motivated?" 265
"How do I fire a salesperson?" 267

PINCHING EVERY PENNY: HOW TO SAVE MONEY IN PLACES YOU NEVER THOUGHT YOUR BUSINESS COULD/273

"How can I get essential marketing-related products and services without spending any money?" 275
"What's the best way to get free promotional materials that work?" 279
"Can I benefit from advertising without paying for it?" 281

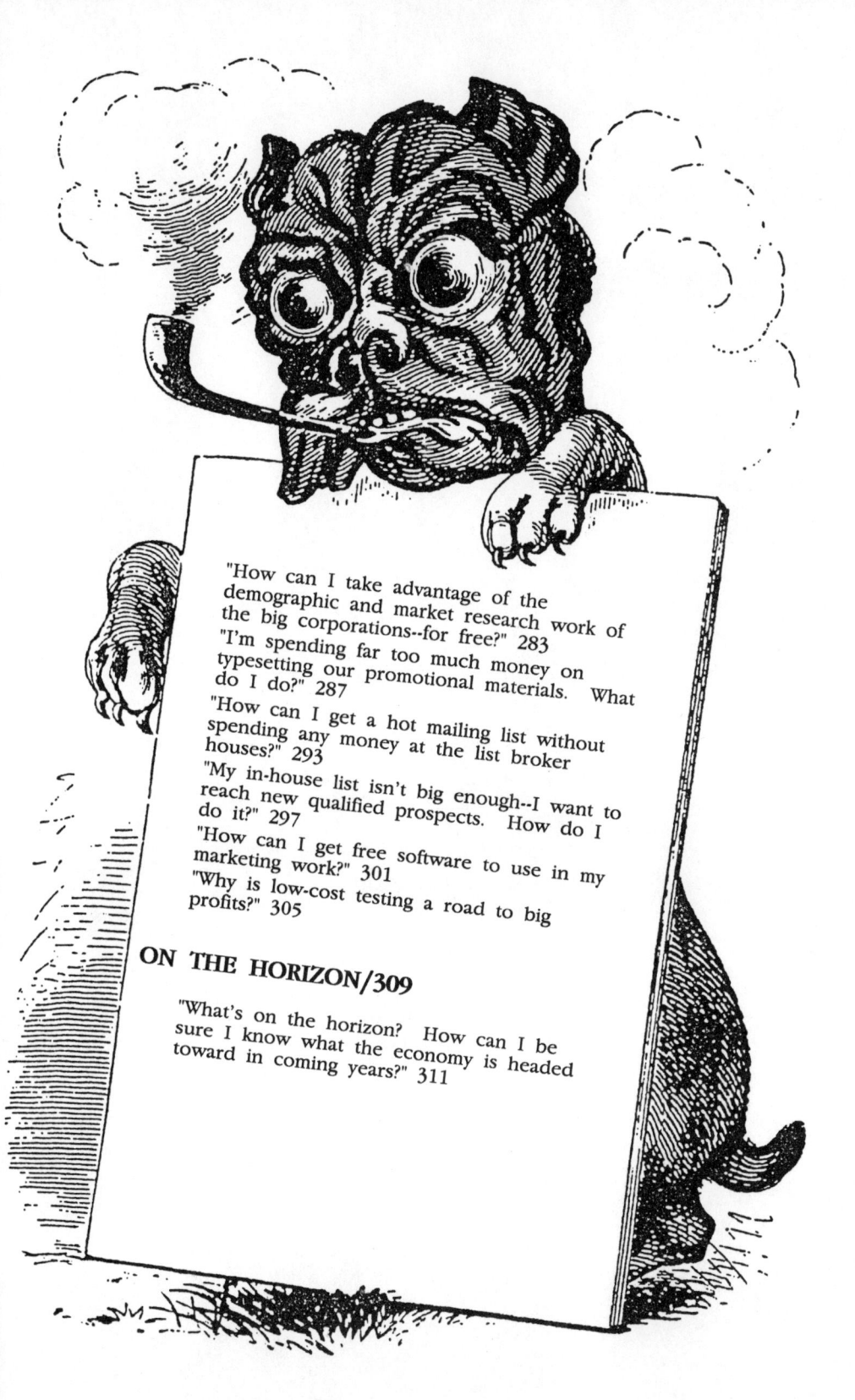

"How can I take advantage of the demographic and market research work of the big corporations--for free?" 283

"I'm spending far too much money on typesetting our promotional materials. What do I do?" 287

"How can I get a hot mailing list without spending any money at the list broker houses?" 293

"My in-house list isn't big enough--I want to reach new qualified prospects. How do I do it?" 297

"How can I get free software to use in my marketing work?" 301

"Why is low-cost testing a road to big profits?" 305

ON THE HORIZON/309

"What's on the horizon? How can I be sure I know what the economy is headed toward in coming years?" 311

PREFACE

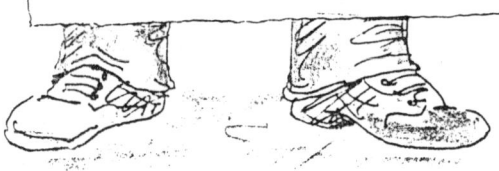

Perhaps you've wondered . . .

"These days, they can even make computers user-friendly, so why are so many marketing books user-hostile?"

If you work in a small or medium-sized business, you want fast help from a marketing book, not long lectures on theory and boring case studies. The book must be concise, and must address immediate concerns. It must answer key questions with workable, cost-effective solutions. It must be easy to read--even if you're pressed for time. Finally, it must offer ideas that you can quickly understand and implement.

This book gives you quick, proven answers. You'll find solutions to the most common marketing problems encountered by businesses like yours--small- and mid-sized operations that can't afford to waste even the smallest amounts of time or money on their marketing efforts.

Emphasis here is on practical ideas you can do yourself, or give to others to do. The accent is not on theory, but on the steps that make sense, are affordable, and are most likely to GET RESULTS.

Where did the ideas come from? The techniques outlined in this book are proven winners from the very highest levels of American business. The reason they're often ignored by smaller firms is not that the ideas are too complex or difficult to carry out . . . but rather that many of the techniques are not widely circulated! By using this book, you can benefit from the experiences of the many, many marketing professionals who have come before you. And you can do it without a "Fortune 500" marketing budget.

Who should read this? This book is for people in small or medium sized units--those who usually have a very limited amount of marketing resources at their disposal. Specifically, it will appeal to people who are in marketing or soon will be, and who want to see the best possible results from their marketing work, regardless of the size of the investment.

What if the reader is in a hurry? Most businesspeople are, and the ideas in this book have been organized with just such readers in mind. The text is designed to be read any way you want. You can go from first page to last. You can scan the table of contents for the answer to a single question that's particularly pressing at a given moment. You can go down the list and highlight only those chapters that seem applicable to your business.

No awards should be handed out for "really" reading the entire text, cover-to-cover (though you might gain a lot of valuable insight from doing so). No penalties need to be imposed for "just" scanning the book for interesting ideas. Each chapter is meant to be free-standing. The book should be considered a tool, not an assignment.

But whether you read the entire book or not, please be sure to TRY some of the ideas suggested. It will only take a couple for you to realize the value of the book you're holding in your hands!

WHY DO I NEED MARKETING?

The answer depends a lot on who's responding. It means different things to different people.

To a salesman, it's personal selling. To an adman, it's ads. A media person will say, "It's media, of course." A professor may have a somewhat more academic definition: the process whereby producers conduct outreach efforts, in an attempt to motivate and persuade purchasers. A production manager may say, "Mostly, it's a lot of nonsense that people get all worked up over for no particular reason!" There is probably no completely authoritative answer: even marketing managers have different definitions. Peter Drucker, one of the world's leading business consultants, says that marketing is "the red line of action between an idea, its delivery, and customer use."

Drucker, accordingly, considers marketing to be THE principal business function. And this view does have its merits. After all, action without communication is like winking at someone in the dark. YOU know what you are doing, but nobody else does.

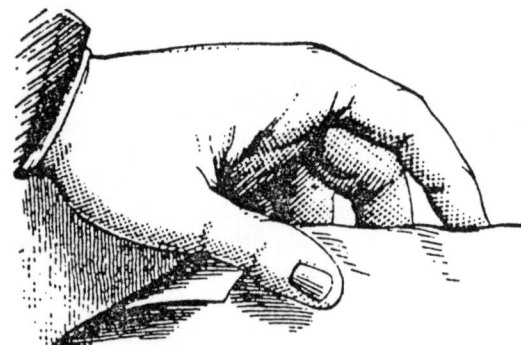

Marketing directors, or others who spend their lives in the profession, will often give you a string of "P's" when asked to define the components of winning marketing efforts: Product, Package, Price, Premium, Promotions, Physical distribution, Personal selling, and Publicity.

A practical working definition might be similar to Peter Drucker's "red line." Marketing cannot exist without an initial product or service idea and its subsequent development. Certainly, marketing must encompass merchandising and sales activities. And, because satisfied customers tend to come back for more (and unsatisfied customers don't), marketers generally can't ignore user perceptions and levels of satisfaction for any length of time. The "red line" idea is reminiscent of the popular C.S.R. (or "Caesar") formula: CONCEPT ... SELLING ... REPURCHASE.

For manufacturers: John Brown has an idea and produces a new model widget. He works with his colleagues and salespeople to develop a telemarketing sales pitch. Customers purchase and even repurchase John's product.

For service industry companies: Mary Smith develops a servicing concept. She runs a modest sales promotion couponing plan. And it works! Customers phone her and she gets repeat business.

For retailers: Bob Jones puts in a new stock of color TVs. He builds some strong in-store displays and shelf promotion items (or "shelftalkers"). The product moves out of the store briskly. Satisfied customers refer others to the store, generating further sales.

If such broad definitions make marketing seem all-encompassing, that's good! Marketing really does affect your entire business. In one way or another, your marketing decisions and actions will have an impact on every stage of your business growth. You may have heard the old saying that nothing really ever happens until somebody sells something. There's quite a bit of truth to it.

This question has many variations: "Can't traffic alone move goods out of my store? If I have a better mousetrap, won't people flock to me automatically? Won't word-of-mouth do the job? I don't really need marketing . . . do I?"

Do you need marketing? The answer is a definite "yes"--unless you fall into one of three extremely narrow categories. 1) If you have a great new breakthrough (perhaps one that solves a major national problem, like a cancer cure), media MAY do your marketing. Then again, it may ignore you completely or give you a thorough and undeserved trashing. 2) If you are lucky enough to have made some sort of guaranteed sale (such as a long term contract), you may not need to reach out for new clients. Beware of the consequences, however, if your "mother account" pulls away unexpectedly! 3) If you really do not want any more sales, it doesn't make much sense to spend time and money trying to reach potential customers. (Some companies actually have too MUCH volume! We should all face such problems.)

The vast majority of small and medium-sized businesses do not fall into any of these three categories. If you do, congratulations. However, if, like most of us, you want increased sales volume, profits, return on investment, and/or personal income . . . then YES, marketing is not only needed, but also probably essential. GOOD marketing, that is--the kind that uses your resources wisely and delivers results.

Remember: you are competing. There are just so many dollars being spent in your product or service category. The "pie" is just so big. You are trying to win a portion. You will never get the whole thing, or even one half. You can try for a slice, though--and so can lots of other people. You're all competing for those slices; some will lose.

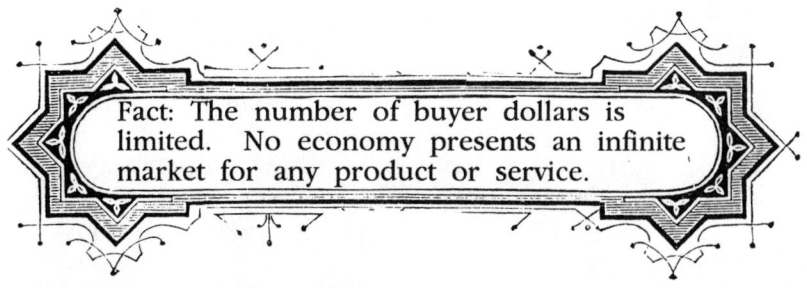

Fact: The number of buyer dollars is limited. No economy presents an infinite market for any product or service.

As a result, many fishermen will be going after the same fish. A few will bite on an un-baited hook, and a few fish will even jump into the boat. This, however, is rare. The fisherman with the best bait and the best methods is likely to catch the most fish.

You are attempting to influence the "hovering hand" you may have heard or read about. The prospective customer has many items to chose from in the market. You are competing for a slice of the pie and a share of his or her mind. More minds equals more hands. More hands equals more profits.

Sure, heavy traffic flow is a big help. More fish are swimming past your boat. Unless you put together some kind of marketing effort, though, they will do just that ... swim right past. You must somehow make prospects WANT to take action.

A "better mousetrap" is important, and so is an improved product; but those are not the only elements of good marketing. You need more to make the sale. How will potential customers know about any product, revolutionary or not, if you keep it a secret, locked away in the cellar or lab? You must find a way to tell others about your good news. Simply telling, however, is not enough. You must tell the news to the right prospects (i.e., heighten your selectivity and efficiency . . . important concerns in most marketing campaigns). And you must communicate to the prospects in such a way that they understand you. Otherwise, you will waste efforts spreading a useless message.

Yes, word-of-mouth can be the best advertising. Shakespeare makes the point that your reputation is usually your most important asset. Ask yourself, though: How does a reputation come about? Who starts the word of mouth? And how does it start? Marketing! It all starts with you. Every word-of-mouth relies on your communication with your prospects to they purchase. And then the word-of-mouth spreads your good reputation. You can (and must!) count on it to spread the good news. You must remember, however, that word-of-mouth doesn't materialize out of thin air.

32   *Marketing Without ...*

Is marketing necessary? It sure is, if you expect to: catch the eye of the potential consumer; win a slice of the market "pie"; influence the "hovering hand"; initiate word of mouth; gain higher sales totals; or dramatically elevate income and profit levels.

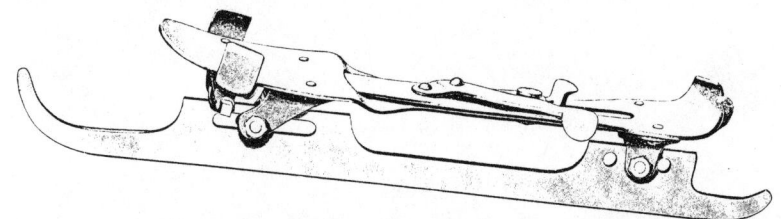

This is an old myth, perpetuated by those who have not had much experience in generating sales. And there is, perhaps, a grain of truth to the idea that gave rise to the myth. People see poor advertising and shoddy products, and conclude that big profits simply happen once a company launches a major campaign.

The real answer is: "Marketing can't sell just anything at a profit indefinitely." If it could, we'd all be selling packaged dirt and living in splendor as a result. Even the most experienced marketers have a very difficult time selling poor products. There is an old saying on this topic among marketing people: "The customer isn't stupid; the customer is your spouse!"

Yes, good marketing will sell some poor products or services. It won't sell enough over time, however, to justify continued ad costs. Keep in mind, moreover, that good marketing often can't even sell fantastic products or services at a profit!

The first step must be a good product or service; that's usually a given in the best marketing work. Quality is essential. Without it, failure is very likely. With it, success is NOT assured, but you're on your way. You've passed the first barrier.

Those who believe that marketing can sell competitively inferior things are enjoying an unrealistic and expensive dream. Try this frightening idea on for size: Good marketing can actually put a low-quality firm out of business faster than poor marketing ... because more people will try the product, and, disgusted, spread negative word-of-mouth.

FIRST STEPS

"Why is quality important--and how do I know when I'm delivering it?"

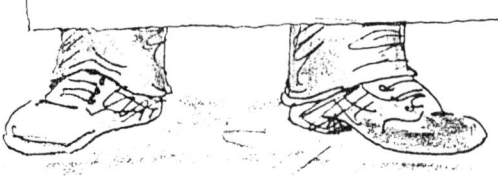

You must deliver a solid value to your customer. That's value determined from the customer's point of view, not yours. If you don't, you are unlikely to prosper in any meaningful way. There are three main reasons to pay very close attention to the way customers perceive the quality of your product or service. High levels of customer-perceived quality will:

Build repeat business.

Encourage positive word-of-mouth (and make all your marketing efforts pay off more).

Protect you from a competitive standpoint.

Note that all that's being suggested is that you deliver SOLID VALUE to the customer, on his or her terms--not the highest conceivable level of quality, regardless of cost. The goal is to engender a positive, "that-was-worth-what-I-paid-for-it" reaction.

It follows, then, that if you're interested in learning whether or not you're meeting the needs and desires of your customers, there's not too much doubt as to who you should be listening to. It won't be any of the highly-touted consultants, authors, or analysts you'll hear talking about the quality challenge on radio or television. Their advice may be helpful, but the final word belongs to your customer. It is to him or her that you must listen most attentively--ESPECIALLY if that customer is angry or upset about something associated with your products or service.

An unsatisfied customer who takes the trouble to tell you what's wrong is the ultimate (free!) consultant. If you find it difficult to listen to customers who are unhappy with your product or service, YOU--not the customer--must change. It's difficult for many to realize, but when someone calls your firm with a complaint, problem, or suggestion, that's a stroke of very good luck! The person is usually alerting you to a problem that many other customers are encountering silently. Listen patiently. Look for ways you can improve. Above all, try to remedy the problem to that customer's satisfaction. If you do, you may be surprised at the loyalty you'll inspire.

"I am a nice customer. I don't complain, no matter how poor the service. I'll sit quietly in a restaurant while people who came in after I did get served ahead of me. In a store, if the salesperson is unpleasant, I say nothing. If some product or service I buy isn't really right, I'm too polite to bring it to anyone's attention. I'm the kind of person who doesn't want to make a fuss. No, I'm a nice customer. And I'll tell you something else that I am. I'm the customer who never comes back."

The absurd (but not uncommon) spectacle of a billion-dollar company that spends vast amounts of money to reach potential customers, but hires a rude or incomprehensible receptionist to greet those prospects, is on the way out. If you make efforts to reach people interested in your product or service, it is senseless to treat their comments to you as an inconvenience. Even if the tone in which the customer's message is delivered is harsh or abrasive, you can usually counteract that. All you have to do is show that you're interested in finding a solution to the problem. Often, when the customer realizes that he or she is talking to someone who wants to help and is willing to see things from the perspective of the end-user, the antagonism melts away instantly!

Listen to your customers! Without them, your business is an irrelevancy.

"Think."

Tom Watson, founder, IBM.

The answer is simple: Think!

Don't rush into anything. Evaluate your circumstances before you set out on a course of action. Time after time, successful small businesses have proven that the wisest philosophy for virtually every situation runs like this: "Think small, think careful, think progressive . . . but think!"

There are thousands of huge firms out there with plenty of dollars to burn but not much in the brains department. All you have to do is succeed with a reversed set of circumstances; lots of strategy and creative risk-taking, and a modest amount of money to spend. (Or, quite possibly, no money at all; as we'll see, there's much you can accomplish, even if you're down to your last dime.)

Think success! Not procedure and bureaucracy. Specifically:

Nurse every nickel. If you're reading this book, you probably don't have too many extra nickels to toss around. Think twice before you make a commitment. Then think twice more. Remember, it's estimated that for every 100 firms that go broke, eighty do so because of poor resource management.

Thought and perspective can help you avoid this trap. Think about the implications of every idea you consider, and don't fall in love with any one initiative. That's romance--not business. If an approach looks promising, that's great. If there are danger signs, heed them.

Realize that you can learn something new. Big companies often fool themselves into thinking they've got the system down pat: "If it ain't broke, don't fix it." Small companies are too close to the ever-changing real world to afford such a fiction. Keep your ears open. You'll find yourself fixing things that are about to break, and taking advantage of opportunities that are about to materialize.

Seek advice from qualified people. Check with your local Small Business Administration and ask about free SCORE (Service Corps of Retired Executives) counselors. Show them your plans. Listen to what they have to say. You may well come across some profitable ideas; you may also be able to avoid some potentially dangerous ones. It's a remarkably good deal. You're under no obligation to follow advice you don't like; all counseling is undertaken in complete confidentiality, and there's no cost to your firm.

Complement your winning strategies with impressive follow-through from every corner of your organization. One good way to do this is to motivate your associates with honest respect and hands-on involvement (another feature lacking in many Fortune 500 work environments). And don't be afraid to offer favorable recognition wherever appropriate. "Get religion" about your business; then try to pass along the winning spirit.

Don't expect miracles. The real world does not, sad to say, beat a path to your door once you build a better mousetrap.

What's more, one good mousetrap ad usually doesn't result in a customer stampede, either. Think about your life, and the way you make your purchasing decisions. It probably takes a little bit of time for you to alter an old habit, or change a brand loyalty. It's the same for your potential customers. Success doesn't happen overnight.

Think positive; be upbeat; be honest; be creative; and work like hell!

"Would you tell me please which way I ought to go from here?" asked Alice.

"That depends a good deal on where you want to get to," said The Cat.

"I really don't much care where..."

"Then it doesn't much matter which way you go," said The Cat.

- Lewis Carroll, ALICE IN WONDERLAND

Making good marketing decisions is similar to making good decisions in any other area of business. Just like Alice in Wonderland, you won't get far if you don't have an objective. Many, if not most, small business failures can be attributed to poor planning and resource management rather than insufficient funding. Fortunately, there are a few steps you can follow that will make planning easier. The entire process is known as "management by objective," and it's been highly effective for many managers and executives. Of course, nothing's guaranteed. There's no such thing as successful decision-making 100% of the time, but these guidelines will help.

How do you manage by objective? Well, you start by making a commitment to put things down on paper. By listing the elements of the main steps (there are three), you can review factors. Change them. Re-arrange them. All without risking a cent. You can put your plan on the back of an envleope, on a legal pad, or on a word processing printout. The main goal is to make the format work for you. Try to be thorough. Orderly. Logical. Readable.

Why should you bother to write the plan? There are two reasons. 1) A well prepared plan gives you considerable clout, authority and strength. If you wish to generate funds from investors or get a loan from a bank, a good plan will be a big help. It will also favorably impress partners, associates, friends, family, salespeople and dealers. 2) More important, it will give you a track to run on: a program, and eventually, a schedule that will outline exactly what to do and when to do it. Here's how it works.

> 1) Define your problem (or: "situation"), and, if you can, your opportunities. Do this carefully; a problem well-defined is often half solved.
>
> Be honest about the circumstances you're facing. This may be difficult, and may require considerable risk on the part of key players in your organization; no one likes to be the bearer of bad news. Nevertheless, it is always best to have access to all the facts, especially the damaging or unflattering ones.
>
> The "5 W's" are a handy device for determining your situation. If you list Who, What, When, Where, Why . . . you'll have a quick summary of the most important information.
>
> 2) Define your goal (or: "objective"). Your objectives describe where you want to go, what you want to accomplish. Typically, they're things like sales volume or profit levels over a given period of time. Don't get confused. Problems or opportunities are not goals, they are the facts we face.
>
> You'd be surprised at how much time is wasted in offices around the country by people who talk a problem in and out, up and down, backwards and forwards--and have no idea what they want out of a given situation. Don't let it happen to you. See if you can condense the goal into one sentence. That way, it can make sense for, and generate results from, a number of people.

In general, the goals you set should be acheivable and yet provide a bit of a challenge. They should be both quantitative (a 10% increase in sales) and quantitative (an improved image among customers. Don't get overprecise; people will not take seriously a request to "increase sales by 10.36%."

3) Define the options open to you (or: "strategies"). What are the ten best ways for you to achieve your objective? Write them down. (If you run out of level-headed ideas, start listing outrageous ones. Some of the best ideas come along when you give yourself some leeway to consider initiatives that might sound silly at first. You can always examine risky strategies at this stage--without committing resources.)

Situation: My sales are low. Objective: Build sales to $1 million. Strategy: use a new in-store promotion, and consider advertising to build customer awareness.

The "8 P's" represent a useful formula for developing your market strategy: Product (or service). Package. Price. Premium. Promotion. Personal Selling. Physical distribution. Publicity. The list offers you a quick run-down of some of the most important areas in which you might want to take action.

4) List the pros and cons (or, in plain English, the advantages and disadvantages) that face you. Be brutally honest about all the drawbacks that accompany a given course of action. Don't just do it in your head; sit down with a legal pad and write them out in two columns. It will make the process much more effective.

5) Don't fly solo. Talk things over with at least one trusted friend, colleague, or professional associate, and preferably two or three.

6) Still stuck? If, after following the steps outlined above, you're still having trouble settling on a course of action, you probably need more information. Get it. There are few problems that can't be put on hold while you gather necessary facts. Some can be put on hold just to be put on hold! (Remember, "doing nothing" is actually an active decision. If you take responsibility for accurately assessing the implications, "stalling" can sometimes be an excellent option.)

7) Have a fall-back position. A workable second approach, just in case things don't work out, has saved many a project. Business is often unpredictable; what makes sense Monday morning may be obsolete by Tuesday afternoon.

When should you plan? All the time. You should always be thinking about next steps, just as a sports coach or combat commander is constantly evaluating tactics. Certainly, one key time to plan is well before any major investment is made. Later may be too late to do anything but count up all the money you've lost.

Because you are competing. Your opposition has spent months, and often years, in preparing. You are trying to win the "votes" or dollars of your prospects. So is the other side. You can't enter that battle without a battle plan and expect to win.

If you are really serious about succeeding in business, and if you are not rich enough to afford considering failure an interesting hobby, then you will want to prepare. The principles are the same as in sports, war, politics, or any other strategic undertaking. You can actually defeat your competitor BEFORE the contest begins--if your planning is markedly superior. America's top companies prove this over and over. Your company can, too.

Case history: A husband and wife team, each former restaurant manager, wanted to start a new business. They studied their prospect audience and concluded there was a need for an "up-scale" food catering service in their area. They checked their probable costs and compared these with their resources. Then they worked out some reasonable sales and profits objectives for a year in advance. They talked to potential customers, and tested several names for their business. Eventually they settled on one that they found to have the widest and strongest preference. They got help and advice from their prospects on product, pricing and delivery service plans. They wrote all this into a plan of several pages. Then-- and only then--did they ask anyone for money or invest any significant sums of their own. The plan greatly impressed investors. It actually helped the entrepreneurs themselves, too. They referred to the plan frequently over the first few months of the business's operation. Of course, the plan was never "finished"--reality stepped in. Certain key points had been misunderstood, and required reassessment. Constant adjustments (part of any business) became common. Eventually, the new business prospered far beyond initial forecasts.

They help keep you from making serious mistakes. Research shows that management "judgment" is right only about 50% of the time. One-half! That means you could get the same results from flipping a coin! You need to slant the odds in your favor. You need hard facts.

Market facts are the radar of smart marketing. A very few dollars wisely invested in this area can often prevent disaster. Bad (read: uninformed) decisions can be catastrophic.

If you know who your prospects are, you are in a much better position to direct your marketing efforts. This may seem like an obvious point, but many firms go out of business because they waste their resources on the wrong target audience.

Find out what they buy. This helps to tell you what to sell ... what product or service to design and offer. Here, as well, mistakes have ruined firms, while good decisions have paid off handsomely.

Find out where your customers can be found. The location: urban or rural? The setting: business or pleasure? The environment: at home, at school, or at work?

Find out when your customers purchase most. What season? What month? Weekday? Weekend? Daytime? Afternoon? Evening? In many business settings, timing really is everything.

Find out why your customers buy. Learn their motivations, their reasons for obtaining an item or engaging a service. This helps in your strategic planning.

Find out who your leading competitors are . . . and the trends for which they're preparing. Are you ready as well? How do you compare with the competition from the customer's perspective? If you offer more than they do (on all fronts), then you are likely to be successful. If you offer significantly less, then you should rethink your approach.

Find out what competitors are saying to your prospects, through personal selling and advertising. If you can say it better, say it louder, or say it in a more compelling fashion, you're probably well advised to do so.

Well, if you make 100% certainty of success a precondition of any decision, you will not get anything accomplished. So relax. Risk is part of the game. Accept it.

Now then. If, after the fact, and having opted for Plan A, you get signals you don't like, your path is actually quite clear. All you do is take a deep breath and go back to the Situation-Objective-Strategy method. Are you really sure you were wrong? Look everything over closely. What is it you really want out of the situation that confronts you now, this morning--not yesterday? What are the pros and cons of the various avenues you can take toward achieving that objective?

If you find you did make a genuine error, then congratulations. You're a member of the human race. Don't castigate yourself endlessly--you're the only you you've got, and you're going to need you! Recognize your mistake. Resolve never to do THAT again. If possible, correct your mistake promptly without trying to cover it up. Start a new plan.

Remember: tomorrow is another day! Keep your perspective. There are people all over the world who have to worry about starvation, calamity, repression, violence, homelessness. You, on the other hand, are lucky enough to be able to worry about how most efficiently to turn a profit through marketing efforts in an economically advanced society. If you make a mistake, life will go on. Smile.

LOTS OF CHEAP IDEAS THAT CAN INCREASE SALES IN A HURRY

You have dozens of low- and no-cost options. They're listed by topic below, complete with helpful page references to the matching sections of this book.

In formulating any marketing plan, shoestring or otherwise, your best bet is to use several approaches. This is referred to as a "marketing mix." When you use such a mix, you don't depend too heavily on any one step. One element, such as a special price, might appeal to one part of your market. A special promotion may be attractive to another part. A mailing might do the job for a third.

No one item is likely to motivate all your prospects. Using more than one step usually puts the odds into your favor.

As a general rule, the main goals are to: 1) communicate with your customers; and 2) be sure that your communication tells them about some added benefit brought by your brand to them.

Here are some ideas for starting points in developing your approach. Each of them are discussed fully in other chapters of this book. You should review them here in order to get an idea of the right "mix" for your firm.

1) Improve your product or service. This usually builds appeal with existing customers, and can offer you a new promotional angle, as well. (See page 39.)

2) Improve your packaging. (See page 73.)

3) Offer a special price. (See page 151.)

4) If appropriate, offer a premium of some sort in exchange for someone's business card. The result: a qualified list of professional (and primarily high-income) prospects. (See page 299.)

5) If appropriate, consider the advantages of a contest or sweepstakes. You needn't spend a great deal to win lots of visibility among consumers. (See page 127.)

6) Stage a simple consumer promotion. Coupons. Rebates. Gifts. Samples. (See page 69.)

7) Improve your personal selling. (See page 237.)

8) Listen to ideas your sales staff may have. (See page 265.)

9) Improve your catalog. (See page 107.)

10) Offer more in-person demonstrations of your product or service. Along the same lines: consider free samples. (See page 77.)

11) Work out a cooperative or shared advertising program with a major retail dealer. (See page 281.)

12) If appropriate, revitalize your in-store displays by using banners, danglers, and shelf-talkers. (See page 81.)

13) Use your in-house list of current customers to your advantage. (See page 293.)

14) Consider a direct mail campaign to past customers. Many may be due to place new orders. (See page 115.)

15) Take advantage of the local and human interest angles you may present to applicable media. Use a strong press release. (See page 85.)

16) Support a local charitable cause, community event, or cultural effort--and gain visibility for your business. People may just remember what they see on the back of the little league jackets. (See page 123.)

17) Organize a contest along the theme: "Why I like your brand." (See page 127.)

18) Target your message to the first-time customer. (See page 103.)

19) Offer special terms for first-time customers. (See page 103.)

20) Solicit dealer suggestions for better marketing. (See page 129.)

21) Study your best competitor. Pick the best steps they use. (See page 133.)

22) Ask customers for prospect referrals. (See page 71.)

23) Listen to customer complaints closely and act on the suggestions you hear. (See page 39 and the pages following.)

24) Use reminder postcards to encourage repeat business. (See page 100.)

25) Set up take-one displays. (See page 101.)

26) If appropriate, consider a "bulletin-board mailing," where you ask the recipient to post a card describing your company and its products, as well as how to order. (See page 98.)

27) Select and work with a good distributor or wholesaler. (See page 135.)

28) Take advantage of free promotional materials. (See page 279.)

29) Try to win favorable media attention. (See page 85.)

30) Make sure you get your fair share of exposure in trade publications and industry newsletters. (See page 93.)

31) Circulate memorable business cards that encourage customer and dealer inquiries. (See page 139.)

32) Use gift certificates to build sales. (See page 143.)

33) Make it easy for the customer to buy from you. (See page 145.)

34) Use networking to boost sales and increase your contacts within your industry. (See page 147.)

35) Make sure your company is represented at industry trade shows. (See page 149.)

36) Make competitive pricing decisions. (See page 151.)

In addition, there are a number of "no-budget" steps you can use to save precious cash, streamline your operation, and make sure your marketing efforts are as efficient as possible.

1) Consider the advantages of bartering and "payment in kind." (See page 275.)

2) Make sure your image among customers (including your company name) is a positive, market-driven one. (See page 119.)

3) Avoid paid advertising (in the Yellow Pages, for instance) until you've established beyond a shadow of a doubt that it's strategically necessary for your firm. Your resources are often best channeled elsewhere. (See page 201.)

4) Take advantage of the demographic and market research work that the major corporations use by noting their marketing and advertising decisions. (See page 283.)

5) Consider the advantages of obtaining a desktop publishing system to cut your typesetting costs. (See page 287.)

6) Use "free" public-domain and voluntary payment software rather than purchasing expensive retail packages. (See page 301.)

7) Use low-cost consumer tests before launching a new product or service. (See page 305.)

8) Hire, motivate, and retain top-quality salespeople. (See pages 257 and 265.)

9) Implement successful marketing and management ideas from the Japanese. (See page 175.)

10) Be prepared for coming trends. (See page 311.)

"What promotions can I use to make business really take off?"

The options, really, are limitless. Sampling. Couponing. Discount offers. It all comes under the heading of "merchandising." The idea is to make an impression on consumers about to make a purchasing decision. Your objective is to influence the "hovering hand" before the customer selects a product or service.

Merchandising builds excitement! And the opportunities are more dramatic than many expect. Those who do not work in marketing rarely think of merchandising at all. They think of marketing as consisting entirely of advertising people and salespeople. Marketing, of course, is a lot more than that; merchandising can be a key component.

How can a small firm use merchandising? Here are some ideas.

1) Check your market. List what your competitors and non-competitors are doing. Can you do that? More important-- can you do it better?

2) List a few programs that look good. Now ask dealers and/or customers to pick their favorite. Don't pre-judge the test. Try the winner on a small scale and see what happens; measure the results.

3) Consider couponing: "This certificate good for 20% off your next widget purchase." Such approaches sell millions of products to millions of people every day. Remember that only a small percentage of coupons are ever redeemed. Typically, redemption rates will be as low as five to ten percent.

4) Think about a refund or premium offer. This is where the customer brings you (or sends you) a proof of purchase in return for a gift, premium, or discount on future purchases.

5) "Account openers" can be great tools; they allow you to offer a special deal or premium to first-time customers.

6) A similar device is the "dealer loader," wherein you offer special terms for larger purchasers such as retailers. It can build sales for both of you!

7) If you're eager to get people to switch from an established competitor, you'll probably want to consider "price-off packs" that combine two items under a legend like, "X cents off!" Pass the savings along to your dealers, if that's applicable.

8) Demonstrate your excellence. Often the best way to generate awareness of your product is to offer free samples (or offer your service on a trial basis).

Ireland
people & places

Irish Brigade - French Army 1745

Miss Jon

oops.

See if you can
beautify (crisp)
it's dark creating
see note have really
something lovely

John + Jacqueline

83, Delaware Hs

Delaware Rd

London W9

England

There are two main approaches you can follow.

The first is the rather straightforward one of offering a discount or rebate to current customers who provide you with the new business of their acquaintances. The logistics of this can vary considerably; certain auto repair shops, for instance, might offer 20% off on a future tune-up after one of their customers "spreads the good word" about the high level of service associated with the mechanics there.

Other businesses might print a message at the bottom of their invoices along the following lines:

"Thank you for your patronage! Enclosed with this invoice you'll find a form requesting information about friends and acquaintances who are also widget users, and who might be interested in our products. Fill it out, return it, and receive a free hand-held calculator with our compliments!"

The gifts you'll actually send as a result of such a campaign will usually be well worth the cost to you. Of course, only a small percentage of the forms will be returned to you--but the information you receive will lead often lead you to high-quality prospects.

The second approach is more relevant to business fields that feature more face-to-face contact: consultants, for instance, or salespeople.

The secret in this area is to avoid the stereotypical, high-pressure requests for new business that most businesspeople encounter far too frequently. Keep your eye on your contact's desires and objectives, and build the relationship first. Then, after a certain level of trust is established, it will be second nature for the person to respond positively to a polite, low-key query about others with whom you might speak.

For further information on this second approach, you may wish to consult the later chapter on networking (page 147).

Packaging represents a tremendous opportunity. That's because in many cases, you don't need a ten million dollar budget to put together a package that's just as effective as anything a Fortune 500 company can assemble--and maybe more effective! If you don't want to take the minimal time and effort necessary to come up with a superior package, you're often better off not trying to sell the product at all.

There's a saying in the publishing industry that, while you can't tell a book by its cover, covers do sell quite a few books. If you are selling any kind of product, you must almost always put it INTO something. It often costs little or nothing more to design the package in an exciting, attractive way than it does to do a no-frills job.

Good packaging attracts and educates. Perhaps most important, it becomes the most indispensable advertisement of all--the one that meets the consumer when he or she is in a position to buy.

TO PUT TOGETHER A TOP-NOTCH PACKAGE, YOU SHOULD:

. . . get a good supplier. Work closely with the firm. Tell your contact that you want a superior package at a reasonable price. Good suppliers like challenges. They have skilled designers who like the chance to create.

. . . show your supplier some samples of the competition. Give them some of your rough ideas. Supply important facts. Identify the themes you want to highlight.

. . . encourage them to come up with A FEW IDEAS. These should be based on your comments in rough (inexpensive) format. Don't ask for one definitive, perfect idea the first time through.

. . . test the various designs in front of dealers or prospective customers. (See the chapter on testing.)

"What about packaging a service, rather than a product?"

Think about the details of your organization. You may not have a "box" for what you do, but you do have people. Their appearance is part of your package. Some service businesses have uniforms, jackets, or dress codes.

You should also pay special attention to the quality of your letterheads, envelopes, and business cards. These items represent low-cost opportunities for your business to shine like the big guys.

Even more important are your brochures and catalogs. These are often all that customers have to go on. Make sure you're getting across the image you want. You'll never know how many customers decide not to do business with you because of poor presentation in this area.

In addition, check your company's approach in personal visits, phone calls, letters, proposals, and forms. Are such contacts professional? Sharp? Uniform?

Your image, in short, must be pleasant, willing, professional, and able. Remember, it doesn't cost much to present a superior "package"--but it can often be quite expensive not to! Don't be fooled by the fact that you usually can't SEE the cost of lost sales in the same way you see a bill that comes to you in the mail. The two types of payments are each quite real. Make sure you present the very best face you can to your customers.

Handing out free samples of your product in a sales environment (i.e., one in which the person can immediately act on a decision to buy your product) can be quite effective for certain types of products. It works best when it's done in person. There are few small-business settings in which free samples by mail will yield encouraging results, so stay on the person-to-person level if at all possible.

About five percent of the people who accept a free sample, typically, will decide to purchase your product right then or at a later date. Those are decent odds. However, there are several "don'ts" associated with free sampling that you should be aware of.

In order to achieve the best possible results . .

Don't ask a person who is rude, unkempt, unclean or unattractive to hand out the samples. (This assumes, of course, that you hire someone to distribute the product, rather than doing the job yourself.) It may sound ruthless, but you will in fact get the best results from an attractive presenter (male or female). Sharp attire also helps. And, of course, the presenter must be polite, confident, and present no hygiene or etiquette problems.

Don't ask people if they want a sample. Just hand them one.

Don't wait for people to initiate a conversation; start right in with the pitch. It might sound something like this: "Good afternoon; we're handing out free samples of Barney's Home Smoked Sausage today-- have some! This sausage has a special hickory seasoning that makes it taste delicious, and it's on sale today for only $1.39 a package."

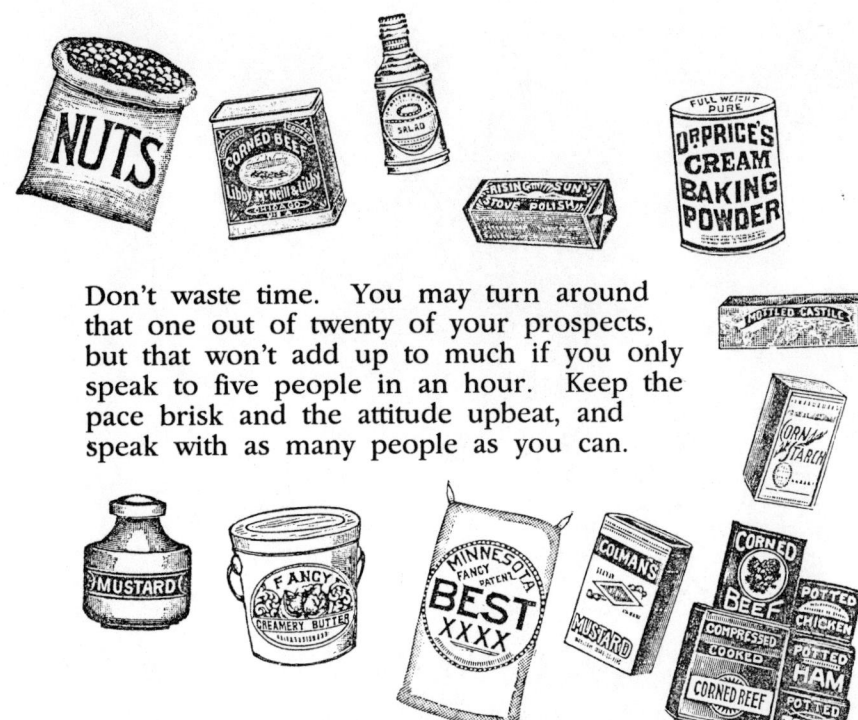

Don't waste time. You may turn around that one out of twenty of your prospects, but that won't add up to much if you only speak to five people in an hour. Keep the pace brisk and the attitude upbeat, and speak with as many people as you can.

... a Marketing Budget

The shelftalker is a small printed piece of paper designed to be fastened to (or hang from) a retail shelf. (It can also work in many non-retail settings.) The unit is designed to take the place of a salesperson, supplying important product benefit information to the potential customer. When well-designed, it can indeed function as a silent sales rep . . . and it doesn't require commission payments or need ego-massaging, either.

Follow the K.I.S.S. formula: Keep It Simple, Stupid! The text on the shelftalker must use ten words or less in total. It's a good idea to keep in mind one of the rules about billboard design forwarded by famed adman Leo Burnett. He asked whether a given message could be seen and understood through a dirty windshield by a driver passing the board at 65 miles per hour on a dark night--during a rainstorm. If it could, the message had a chance to reach its audience. If it could not, it was a waste of money.

Consumers may not be driving down your aisles in go-karts, but they do have a lot of distractions to deal with. Make it easy for them. Don't go into a lecture about your company's history, philosophy, personnel policies, or anything else on the shelftalker. Stick with the basics: lower price, new product, better results.

Tie the shelftalker to the product with parallel design elements. If the package is green, your shelftalker should probably be green. You should strongly consider using a high-quality photo or illustration of the product.

You must mention the product name on the shelftalker. Many of these pieces are designed poorly, highlighting a benefit that the prospect is unable to connect to a given product. (For example, "FIFTY CENTS OFF!" without a photo or any accompanying text.) Leave no doubts about your product's identity and benefit. Make it easy for your customer. And be sure to highlight the benefit in a dramatic way. You will, quite literally, be fighting for the attention that you can win in the blink of an eye.

Shelftalkers that bob, bounce, or dangle have been shown to deliver better results than those that are simply fastened to a shelf. Consider working with your printer to develop a cost-effective model that will work for you.

It's a decent bet that what you're really after isn't just free publicity, but favorable free publicity. The distinction is important, though there are those who argue that even negative press counts as exposure and can benefit you. There may be some truth to the old adage about not caring what the press writes as long as they spell your name right. Nevertheless, given the choice, we all prefer rave reviews to pans.

Favorable media attention is comparable to free advertising--only it's better! People tend to believe news reports more easily than advertisements. In the right setting, belief translates to action, and action is what you want. In addition, news and editorial features typically receive twice the readership of advertisements. (When you read your morning paper, do you skip the feature articles to get to the ads, or vice versa?)

How does it happen? Usually from a reporter's own initiative (which you can't control) or as a result of a press release (which you can). Strong press releases can be extremely useful and inexpensive tools in your marketing efforts. Here are some guidelines you should bear in mind in putting yours together.

Don't write an ad. It's the surest way to make sure your press release is sent immediately to the "circular file."
See things from the editor's perspective. The item must be newsworthy for it to receive serious consideration. That doesn't mean your press release always has to concern itself with summit conferences or arms reduction talks, but it does mean that whatever you put forward must be of genuine interest to the readers or viewers the editor is trying to reach. That interest can be defined in a number of ways. Usually, it describes the presence of either a) some emotional reaction to the story in question; or b) a real-life, practical application of the information you have to offer.

Expect only brief or casual mention of your company, products, or services. Remember: editorial material has much greater impact than ad copy. A little will go a long way.

Keep it short. Get to the point in an honest, interesting way--in one page. Making it any longer jeopardizes your chances of being "picked up." Editors are busy people, with many more important things to do than study unsolicited press releases. They're more likely to scan your material the first time through than read it. So make the most of the limited time you have.

Keep it standardized. White paper. Pica or elite ("typewriter style") typeface--even if you use a word processor. Contact information, including phone number, at the top.

Keep it timely. It's hard to get excited about the wonders of a "new" product that came out six months ago. Editors live by the saying, "There's nothing older than yesterday's news."

Send photos if you can, particularly to the visually-oriented television media.

Start with a lead paragraph that grabs the reader.

"Your drinking water may contain unacceptable levels of pollutants--impurities that often escape the notice of state and federal authorities."

"Are you a man under the age of 25? Then you're probably paying far more for your car insurance than members of any other group."

"Do you remember what television program you watched last night? The major television networks don't think so; a new study commissioned by the broadcasters, recently released as a paperback, reveals that 55% of the nation's viewers have little or no retention of the content--or even titles--of prime time television shows."

Start small--you have an automatic "in" at the papers, magazines and stations in your area. You're a local! Use that fact to your advantage . . . and work your way up.

If possible, deliver your release personally-- rather than by mail.

SAMPLE PRESS RELEASE:

FOR IMMEDIATE RELEASE

For further information contact Jacob Johansen, Martin Enterprises, 617/555-1212. Mailing address: 480 Winter Street, Cambridge MA 02138.

Are these questions illegal?

"Do you prefer to be addressed as Miss, Ms., or Mrs.?" "Where were you born?" "How old are you?" "How old are your children?" "What is your native language?"

If you are interviewing for a job they are.

How can an interviewee tell when he/she is being asked an illegal question? How should they be handled? Under what circumstances should an interviewee file a discriminatory suit against a company?

Employment expert John Martin has advice on this and a number of other provocative issues concerning the job interview. "Often," Martin notes, "discriminatory questions appear to be so innocuous that the candidate does not realize that he/she is being probed for information that is not relevant to his/her ability to do the job."

Mr. Martin also has strong and controversial opinions on drug testing and lie detector tests. In addition, he offers pertinent advice to those who are morally opposed to such tests with advice on how to say "no" to drug tests without losing the job.

JOHN MARTIN, president of Martin Resources, offers resume and career counseling advice to all levels of job seekers in the greater Indianapolis area, and is engaged in a number of management training consulting projects. He has taken part in numerous seminars and workshops across the country on personnel and hiring issues. His dynamic personality and engaging manner have made him a highly sought after lecturer and talk-show guest.

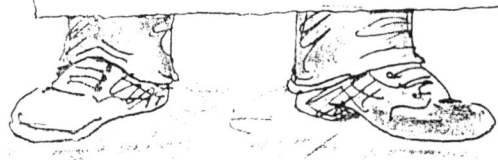

Congratulations. Now comes the tough part.

Above all else, don't ramble. Keep your discussion about your products or services firmly rooted in the topics that are of interest to the show's audience. Wherever appropriate, tactfully mention your product and company, and perhaps some contact information. Don't subject the host or the audience to a blatant sales pitch. It will lead to a strained atmosphere, and you won't be invited back.

Rehearse with friends beforehand if at all possible. If you think such roleplaying will make you uncomfortable, try anyway. You'll almost certainly be far MORE uncomfortable and nervous when you're on the air!

Compose a list of ten pertinent questions about you, your company, and your work--again, being careful to keep in mind the audience's level of interest in the topics. More often than you might imagine, the host will ask you the questions word for word, and thank you after the show for doing the legwork!

Keep your responses short and interesting. Have you ever been cornered by a real "windbag" at a social gathering? It's an unpleasant experience. When you're watching television, the situation is considerably easier to handle. You just change the channel.

After the show, write short, personalized "thank-you" notes to your contacts at the station. Better yet, get audience members to write, complimenting the management on their selection of such a fascinating guest!

We're talking here about the specialized journals and periodicals that may have comparatively low circulation numbers, but reach high percentages of a given field's professionals or decision-makers. Your local library can help you identify the titles most pertinent to your business. VARIETY, for instance, is a trade publication read by those active in the entertainment industry. PUBLISHERS WEEKLY is a trade publication read by booksellers and those active in the publishing field. There are many, many such outlets, some for fields so narrow you might not think anyone would bother to write them in the first place. But write they do, and even the most unlikely titles can carry considerable clout with a given audience, whatever its size.

There's seemingly no limit to the number of specialized trade and professional publications in existence today. Each has a super-qualified, remarkably loyal audience. It's hard to imagine a business that would not benefit by reaching the readers of at least one of these publications. Whether you're trying to highlight your standing among peers, or you want attract the attention of a certain category of potential customers, you have nothing to lose--and everything to gain--by assembling press releases and media packages for key "insider" publications.

It's true: keeping industry journals abreast of your success is one of the most cost-effective publicity options available. You can gain broad exposure to a key audience, usually at no cost to you. Yet many smaller firms do not take advantage of the opportunities that trade publications present!

How do you get the trade publications to notice you? The basic rules for assembling a press release, covered elsewhere in this book, still apply. However, the odds are a little more favorable from your perspective-- if you target your materials correctly. The good news is, if your business relates directly to the readership of the publication, you won't have to worry quite as much about a "hard news" angle. A press release on a new breed of sheep you've imported will not make much difference to the business editor at the New York Times; but it will be much more likely to catch the eye of the features editor of The Monthly Sheep Gazette.

These publications are often hungry for new material. That can work very much to your advantage, but you must still refrain from the blatant sales-pitch style of writing.

Hucksterism pervades much of the mail that crosses any editor's desk, and it is an excellent reason to throw away unsolicited requests for coverage. Make sure you're thinking like the editor. How will the readers of the publication benefit from the information you're hoping to have circulated? Is the opening paragraph a "grabber"? Does the material stay away from concepts the audience will find biased, complicated, or uninteresting?

Include photographs if you can; these will heighten the visibility of your mailing and increase the likelihood of a positive response from the editor. If the photos are used in the final layout, all the better.

As with other media, you should be prepared to see only passing mention of your product or service. That's not bad at all. Remember that any editorial mention in a trade publication is likely to be read--and trusted--by members of the target group you've selected. Such publicity carries much more impact than paid display advertising!

"Can I build sales with only a ream of letter-sized paper and some three-by-five cards?"

There are three excellent (and seldom-used) techniques requiring these simple tools that can yield dramatic, positive results for your business. Each requires a little ingenuity and perhaps a measure of patience, but each can help you increase profits at virtually no cost. (Some of the advice below will probably be easier to carry out with a personal computer and an office copier. If you don't have access to these, however, and don't mind a little more manual work and a trip to the local copy shop, they'll still work.)

Note on the materials: It's best to use unlined three-by-five cards . . . and it turns out to be quite important to choose the right color. Make sure the cards are orange. Research has proven this to be a true "action" color, preferable by far to any other shade. If printing through a word processor, you will probably want to obtain continuous-feed cards that can be run through your daisywheel or ink-jet printer. Unfortunately, continuous-feed orange cards are not as easy to find in the local stationery store as one might like. If you can't track down a supplier, contact System Support Data, at 1022 Morrissey Boulevard, Boston MA 02122. The phone number is 617/288-9840. They'll be able to get you an adequate supply of the cards at a reasonable price. Avoid, at all costs, using standard white index cards. Remember: the cards must be orange!

Idea One: The Bulletin-Board Mailing. I developed this approach while marketing a fairly expensive medical reference text; it worked spectacularly. The technique is most useful when you're undertaking a direct-mail campaign that will reach decision-makers who are exposed to a large number of other people likely to use your product. Librarians or counselors, for instance, would fall into this category. As with any direct-mail campaign, the profits will, as a general rule, be better for high-priced items, and worse for low-priced ones, due to the low overall response rate.

Here's what you do.

STEP ONE: Compose a simple handbill describing your product, with ordering information (perhaps in a coupon). Prominently include something like the following phrase: "For your convenience, we have included a handy card for easy reference by your widget users. Please post it on your organization's bulletin board." (The "convenience," of course, is that the addressee won't be pestered by widget users asking about how to obtain your product.)

STEP TWO: Condense the material on the handbill, and place it, with a short, striking headline, on the three-by-five card.

STEP THREE: Staple the card, on its far left or far right edge, to the handbill, near the middle. This will allow it to be removed easily.

STEP FOUR: Fold the handbill into thirds, so that the printed side is inside and the blank side is exposed. The handbill should now resemble an envelope, which is exactly what you'll be using it for; tape it shut, write your return address and the address of the person you want it to reach, and mail it. With a decent in-house prospect list (and good design and copywriting), you'll end up with orders from your addressees in the short term--and from bulletin-board readers in the long term!

Idea Two: The Reminder Postcard. Many businesses can heighten repeat business by informing customers of an impending deadline. Dentists, for instance, often inform patients that it's time for their next checkup. Mechanics remind car-owners that the next scheduled tune-up is due on a certain date. How do they remind customers? With a postcard! You may be able to use this technique to your advantage. Use the index cards and your word processor to develop a simpler reminder postcard. It will prove especially effective if you can highlight a date by which a certain program or discount must be requested.

Idea Three: Take-One Displays. Is there a location your potential customers frequent to which you might gain access? A movie lobby, for instance, or a reception area? If so, you can assemble a simple "take-one" display with a small box, a standard letter-sized sheet of paper, and your index cards.

You might decide to take the simplest route: printing a legend like "Widget Users-- Take One" in huge letters on the sheet.

"How can I target the first-time customer--and get the person to come back for more?"

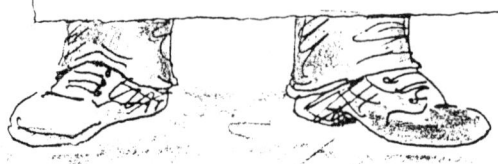

This is one of the most frequently asked questions in any business, and one or two pages on the topic here is not going to give you anything resembling a definitive answer. Still, there is one approach you should consider in trying to attract and retain first-time customers.

When you mount a high-visibility campaign of any sort, expensive or low-budget, be absolutely certain that you can deliver top-notch, high-quality service with a smile. This may seem like an obvious point, but there are many businesses that put together huge promotional budgets and far-reaching ad campaigns, hoping to draw in new prospects, only to have the majority of those prospects make "one-time-only" appearances. Why? Because the customers were subjected to rude salespeople, a hectic atmosphere, unattractive displays, or unacceptable levels of merchandise stockouts.

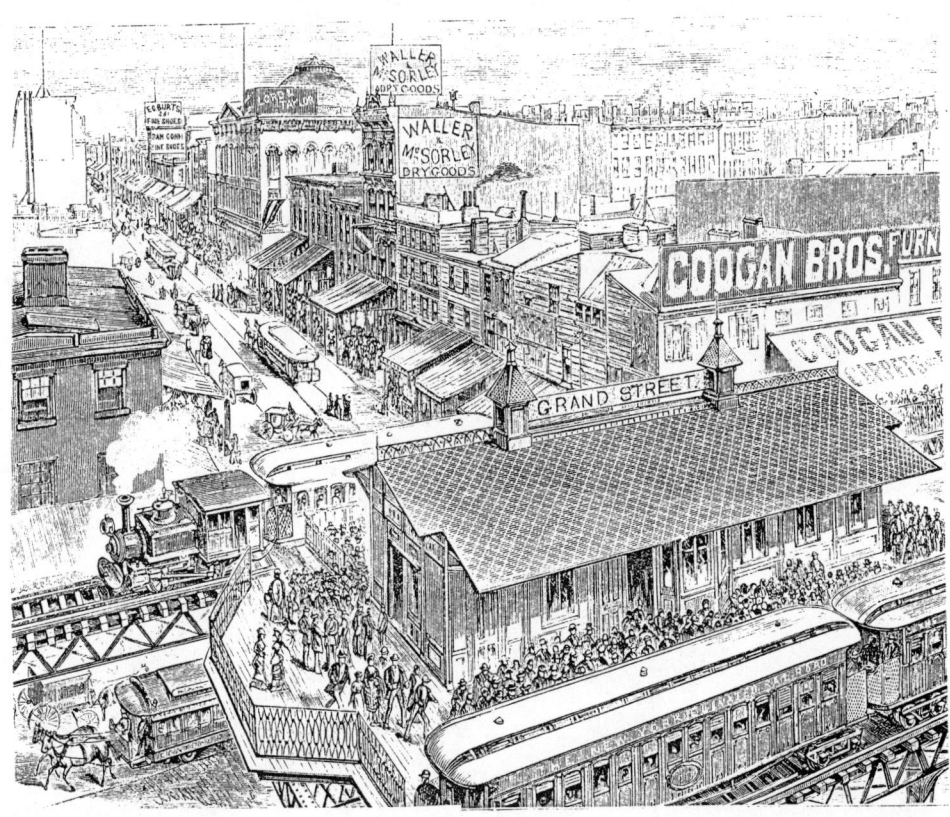

Many "people-oriented" firms (particularly restaurants, which live or die by word-of-mouth recommendations) have found a way around this problem. Here's how they do it. They open their doors to the public, but make no effort to gain any kind of media attention, free or paid. In short, they conduct no outreach efforts at all--for two or three months. Over that period, they work all the kinks out of their organization. They learn where organizational problems exist, where responsibilities lapse or overlap, and what exactly is likely to result in the main thing they want to avoid: an unsatisfied customer.

Then, after this trial period, they announce their Grand Opening (or big spring sale, or singles night, or other promotional event), and invite the media in to take a look--or perhaps they take out paid advertisements. That way, they don't actively lobby for curious (and highly impressionable) new customers until they know the service level is superior.

You have only one opportunity to make a good first impression with your customer. Make sure the inquisitive first-timer is getting your very best shot. If you have doubts about the levels of service your employees are providing, there is an excellent way to settle those doubts. It's called the "mystery customer" technique. That's where you find a friend or relative unknown to your employees, and ask that person to pretend to be a first-time customer. See what kind of treatment the "mystery customer" gets on walking into your facility. If some of your people did well, congraulate them. You might even consider some sort of bonus or gift certificate as an incentive. But if there are problems, you'll know exactly what kind--and, after you discuss the matter with your people, they'll probably have a renewed respect for unfamiliar faces.

Your objective is consumer interest, excitement, and above all,

ACTION!

You want people to look at your catalog and think, "Wow!" this is a great company! This is just what I want!"

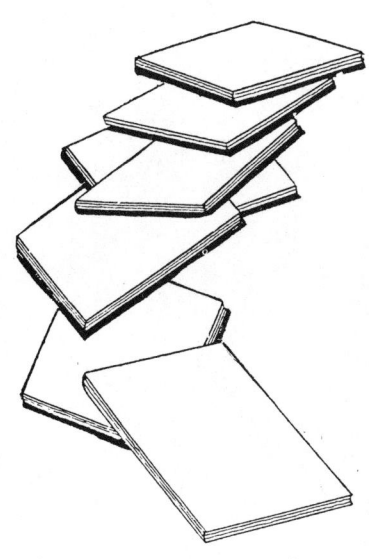

The catalog is, for most businesses, a key tool in the marketing arsenal. In many businesses, it's the only tool! So it's crucial to get the most impact possible out of your catalog. It must reach your potential customer, command attention, and inspire action. In short, it must work as a giant, super-effective ad. As such, its development will present many challenges and opportunities.

The catalog is not a "laundry list" of your products or services. Simply listing the information in a dull or unprofessional manner will not generate sales. Why should it? Would a crumpled, scrawled note left on your desk, on its own, convince you to drop what you're doing, run out, and suddenly make a major purchase like a car or a tractor?

You must first make the potential customer care. Then supply the necessary information in an interesting manner that shows all the ways you meet the prospect's needs or desires. Then get the person to take action.

The cover is vitally important, and must serve as the "grabber of all grabbers," the lead-in by which your efforts will stand or fall. If the cover is uninteresting or poorly designed, the best writer in the world won't be able to compensate for your resulting loss of audience. Consider a striking photograph or bold graphic design. Highlight interest in your product and its benefits.

Establish a primary goal you'd like your catalog to achieve. What would you like to do? Open doors? Build new sales? Generate inquiries? Build your reputation? Build on past success, and translate that into more repeat customers? Whatever it is, keep that goal in mind as you design your material.

Use the million dollar checklist (see page 217) for all copy you use in your catalog. Test your copy. If the results indicate you have more work to do, start over again. Try to compose your catalog well ahead of any pressing deadlines (for instance, a major convention) so that you have plenty of time to come up with and refine your ideas.

Keep the reader's perspective in mind at all times, and never lose sight the manner in which your catalog is likely to be distributed. For instance, will you mail the literature to people who've never heard of you? If so, how will you have to adjust your style?

If you use one, be fussy about the design of your order form. The order form's importance is frequently underestimated. Too often, the result is lost sales. This is where your customer decides what to buy! For goodness sake, don't ask him or her to do business with you on the basis of a cramped, ill-organized, graphically awkward form. Make things easy: large, legible type; clear, flowing design; unmistakable instructions geared toward action.

Well before you complete production, find a good printer. Your ideal candidate will be someone who's willing to work with you in selecting paper stock, cover finish, and binding methods--and offer competitive rates.

Last--but not least--pass it around. Your catalog will probably represent a substantial investment of time and money. It may even singlehandedly determine your company's rate of success for an extended period of time. With so much at stake, don't take the chance of finalizing format, content, or page length decisions until you've received plenty of input from people you respect. Chances are, your associates or colleagues will unearth a few problems you'll be glad to have the chance to remedy.

# "We don't use catalogs--our emphasis is on handbills and flyers. Something that simple is hard to mess up, isn't it?"

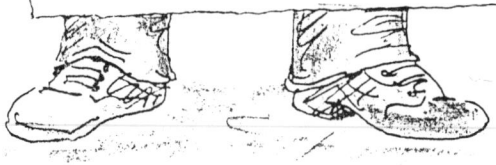

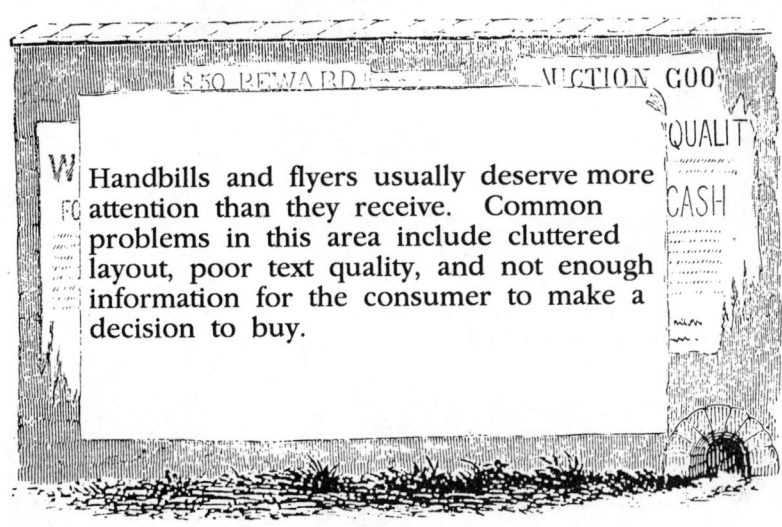

Handbills and flyers usually deserve more attention than they receive. Common problems in this area include cluttered layout, poor text quality, and not enough information for the consumer to make a decision to buy.

These pieces are usually given out in public or placed in mailboxes. They should contain a strong statement of product or service benefits, an illustration or photo, strong selling points, and--most important of all--information on how to follow up on the interest that's been created. A related marketing tool is the selling sheet. This is typically distributed to retailers, and highlights the benefits awaiting them (almost always increased profits) through use of a product or service.

Handbills and selling sheets, just like "regular" ads, should be measured against the Million Dollar Checklist (see page 216).

The main difference between this form of promotion and other types of advertising is its immediacy. Handbills, flyers, and selling sheets, as a general rule, demand the use of a phone number or address for the reader to consult in making the next "action" step.

These types of promotions often end up in someone's pocket or notebook--because your product or service is so interesting that the receiver wants to get back to you later! Make it easy for him or her to do so.

Successful selling sheets contain: only information of interest to the audience (i.e., retailers); a strong emphasis on increasing profitability; proof of claims and supporting information (test results, ad dates, and so on); specific future promotional plans; and suggested initial stocking levels.

In both handbills and selling sheets, you should not be afraid to conclude your copy by telling the reader what to do. Examples: "Order now!" "Call 555-1111 today!" "Keep plenty on hand!" No one has ever passed a law against asking for the sale. Try it.

Direct mail has many pros and cons. The main disadvantages: it takes a lot of work; it can be comparatively expensive to reach any given customer; and it relies on mailing lists, which you must usually purchase from outside vendors, and which quickly become obsolete. The main advantages: it can be highly "targetable," reaching only prospects in specific categories; it is versatile, allowing you to reach a large or small audience as you see fit; and it can have more impact than a print ad, because even busy people usually glance through all their mail--though they will often pass over, say, a newspaper advertisement without a second look.

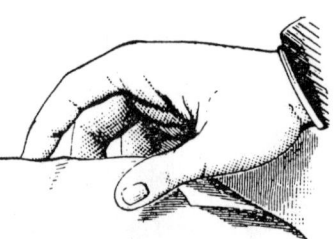

If you're selling one product, one time, at a relatively low cost, direct mail may not be for you. On the other hand, higher-ticket items, or special-offer campaigns designed to win new customers, can perform better. This has to do with the low response rates associated with this kind of marketing.

A "good" direct mailing will generate inquiries from between one and two percent of the list you use. Obviously, this can vary tremendously, but the pattern should be clear.

If you want to sell mini-widgets through direct mail at $2.95 each, you're probably going to have a hard time doing it. No matter how big your initial list, you will probably be unable to generate enough responses to cover the postage, the printing, and the cost of the list. On the other hand, if you want to sell full-size electric widgets through direct mail at $24.95 each, you might be able to accomplish something with a one percent response rate. And the scenario might look even better if all you wanted out of the arrangement was a few responses from potential customers who could come back again and again to your widget shop, thereby justifying, over time, your initial investment in the mailing.

Of course, it's essential to have a good mailing list, one that offers you widget users and only widget users, so you don't waste time mailing pieces to people who won't do business with you. Remember, one of the big advantages of direct mail is efficiency--but you have to make it happen! Don't buy a list composed of, say, "residents" of your town unless every single person actually has a genuine need or interest in your product. (A rare circumstance.)

Watch your own mailbox. Every piece of "junk mail" you receive is something that took money to design, produce, and mail. Does a certain piece attract your interest? Get you to open it? Motivate you to make a purchase? Why? Keep notes; try to reproduce successful techniques, adding your own ideas and product/service angles.

Choosing your firm's name is one of the most important marketing decisions you will make. Don't make it rashly. Your name is the first thing customers, industry observers, salespeople, media professionals, and a host of other important people will have to judge you by. If it's complicated, imprecise, or amateurish, you will be sabotaging everything else you do. Your name determines, to a large degree, what kind of first impression you'll leave. Everything else you do will be affected by it.

There are distinct advantages to getting it right the first time. For one thing, if you decide you must change your name a year or more down the line, you'll probably face the considerable inconvenience of modifying many internal items. All your stationery, invoices, promotional materials, and records will list the old name. But that extra work seems like nothing when it's compared to the confusion and wheel-spinning you'll face in dealing with customers, creditors, vendors, and banks, to name just a few. All of these people will have come to know you by the original (ill-chosen) name.

Changing your company name, in many ways, means starting a new company. You'll be abandoning a good portion of whatever goodwill and positive image you've built up. Don't do it unless you can avoid it. If you can't avoid it (and many companies can't), then make sure the replacement name is a real winner.

Common mistakes people make in naming companies include: naming it after the boss's kid (Jennifer Septic Works); choosing a hackneyed or commonplace name (ABC Towing, Acme Rentals); naming the company after the proprietor if his or her name is difficult to read or pronounce (Brzenskikov Florists); and choosing names that have negative or confusing overtones (Deadly Accurate Precision Grinding, Stone Rubber Company).

Major corporations often spend large sums of money finding just the right name. No one set of standards will apply to every company, but the best advice on name selection applies to big firms and small ones alike. Test, test, and re-test. Come up with between twelve and twenty possible names, then show them to potential customers, media people, and professional colleagues. See what comes out on top.

Consider strong acronymic names (JJ Resources), humorous names (Humphrey Go-Karts), or one-word compounds (TypeWorks), all of which are currently popular approaches. Does your name target your business to a specific customer group? Leave you enough room to expand to a new field later on? Stick with people after one hearing? Conjure up the appropriate image?

"What are the best low-cost ways to build my company's visibility within our community?"

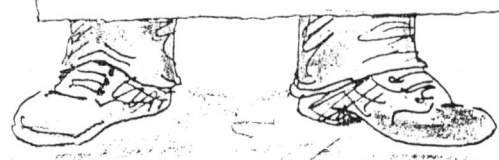

There are two main approaches, and each can yield excellent long-term results. Good community relations can be a cornerstone of your successful business strategy. It is usually well worth the minimal time and effort it entails.

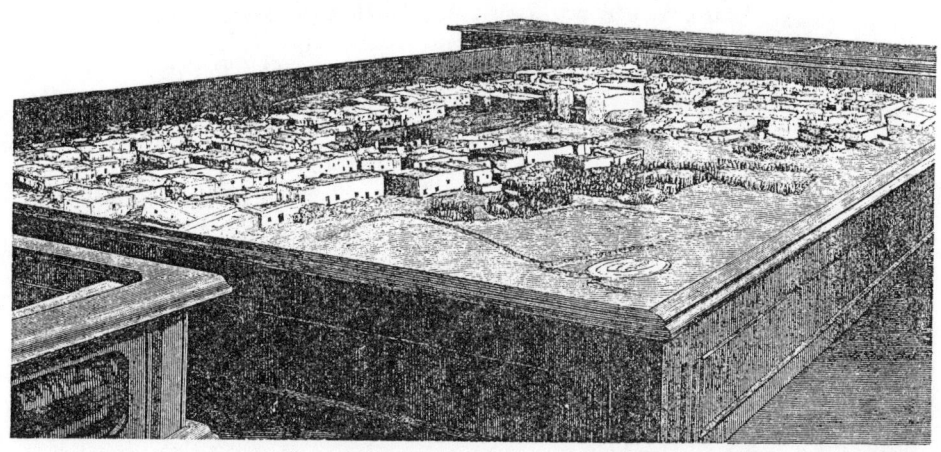

One popular approach is to sponsor a charitable organization or community project. Buying uniforms for the local little league team is a popular option, and can prove especially effective for companies that desire higher local name recognition. Your logo or slogan, of course, should be prominently displayed on the uniform.

Other options might include participation in a local redevelopment or recreational project such as a playground or daycare center, or high-visibility donations of goods or services to the local public television or public radio station. ("Make a donation of $25 to WZZZ and receive a certificate for 10 widgets from Ted's Widget Shop in Anytown!") These gifts to nonprofit broadcast outlets, used for fundraising purposes, can offer you remarkably cost-efficient exposure for your business--and build your reputation in the community, as well. (It will also make up for all those years you watched UPSTAIRS, DOWNSTAIRS without writing a check at pledge time.)

Another good idea is to work hard at instilling a sense of community spirit among your employees. Many larger firms do this with great success, and some of these programs inspire intense loyalty from the residents of the cities and towns in which the firms do business.

Mutual of Omaha, for instance, located in Nebraska, sponsors a much-admired program promoting employee involvement in charitable and community causes in the Omaha area. The efforts extend to every single one of their over 4000 employees, who are regularly singled out for awards and company recognition for particularly notable contributions to the community. The approach can be rewarding for your business as well.

Did you ever notice how many contests the major corporations run in conjunction with a product? "Win a trip to Disneyland!" "Win a brand new car!" There's a reason these are so popular. When publicized correctly, such promotions can build sales dramatically. The fact that a winner is chosen at random for some prize, after all, is an exciting thought for many people. It means each participant has nothing to lose--and a lot to gain--by taking part in the promotion.

You're probably not in a position to give away any Rolls-Royces. However, you might consider contests if your goal is to build awareness and excitement. Vacations to popular resort locations are a relatively inexpensive prize that can bring high visibility.

A basic display is relatively simple to set up. You can follow the examples you're likely to see in any supermarket, drugstore, or other high-traffic retail outlet--or you can opt for a simple poster above a box designed for collection of entry blanks. The display should incorporate a solid, striking design that prominently features the prize to be given to the lucky winner. Good quality photographs or drawings are recommended. A tear-off coupon is also helpful.

A topic for your contest that's proven quite successful over the years is to ask contestants to write something on the topic, "Why I like ABC Widgets."

It's a good idea to discuss your promotion with your attorney before you finalize any plans. Guidelines on contests and promotions will vary from state to state, and you may face some restrictions in the way you can conduct this type of program.

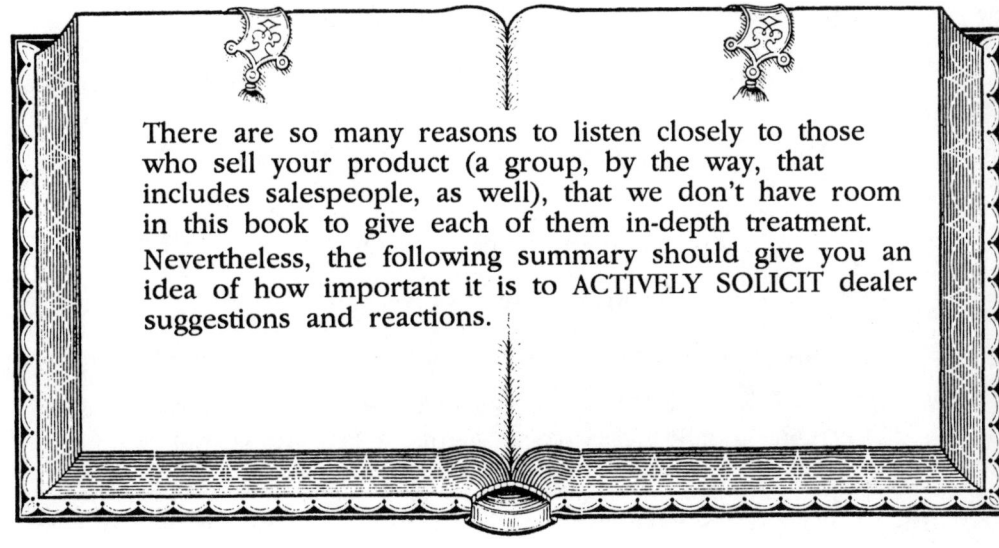

There are so many reasons to listen closely to those who sell your product (a group, by the way, that includes salespeople, as well), that we don't have room in this book to give each of them in-depth treatment. Nevertheless, the following summary should give you an idea of how important it is to ACTIVELY SOLICIT dealer suggestions and reactions.

They know what your competition is doing.

They know what customers like.

They know what customers don't like.

They're aware of hot trends and sudden reversals.

They have a good eye for the promotions that will pay off.

They appreciate being kept informed about your plans.

They can tell you when someone else has tried and failed to do what you're considering doing.

They can tell you why they failed.

They usually don't have an ax to grind--other than a desire for higher sales.

They can alert you to problems with your product quality.

They often have excellent ideas for new products or services.

Of course, you shouldn't endlessly pester people who work hard to get your products into the hands of customers. However, an occasional polite phone call to key accounts is often an invaluable aid.

"How can competitors' ads help build my sales?"

Whether you advertise or not, you should keep a close eye on the advertisements of your competition. They'll clue you in to themes, selling points, media selection, market orientation, overall strategy, and a whole host of other important tips.

How will you know whether or not the material is even worth reviewing? What if the competition makes a mistake? The best approach is to be selective, and not to leap to conclusions before you see a clear pattern emerging. Watch your most successful competitors, not the failures. Keep your eyes and ears open. Somebody who is in your business is paying to say thus-and-such to your potential customers. Don't you think you should know what's being passed along?

Assemble a simple scrapbook of competitors' ads as they run. Date the entries. Keep it accurate over time. Possible sources might include local newspapers, mail, broadcast ads, and billboards. By clipping and pasting a few ads over a period of time, you'll assemble a valuable tool that will help you market your own product or service--whether or not you decide to advertise! Keep a section of the scrapbook open to record your own observations: "Dealers say this ad really bombed . . ." "The three biggest groups they're reaching are . . ." "They've identified X as a major selling point . . ."

Watch for repeats, especially if you do decide to advertise. An ad that runs continually is working. Noticing that ad is just like getting an update on strategy from your competition saying, "Hey, we've got something here. This one's tried, true, and profitable." The ad is tested at their expense, not yours--and you get the good news!

In addition, keep an eye out for non-advertising messages your competition may be sending. List two or three of your best competitors, then get on their mailing list. You should also watch media outlets, especially newspapers, for free publicity (favorable or otherwise) your market rivals may receive.

Procter & Gamble, one of the very best marketing organizations in the world, has a comprehensive program for gathering the advertisements of competitors. An agency working with the firm must review these carefully and submit written comments--comments that come in very handy when it's time to prepare new advertising, promotion, or product design strategies.

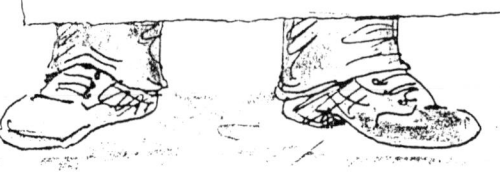

A distributor or wholesaler is an organization that buys from or represents a manufacturer, and then sells to retailers.

When do they serve you best? When your product is already well established and available throughout the market. Most successful relationships are initiated after a steady demand for a given product has already been established. At that point, the manufacturer cannot possibly afford to contact the thousands of small and medium sized retailers that wholesalers or distributors can.

One of the most common small-business misconceptions is that these organizations will actively go out and sell a manufacturer's line. This rarely happens. Wholesalers and distributors are, broadly speaking, order takers. Though they will often remind a retailer, through newsletters or checklists, of certain products, they cannot be expected to take much initiative in building up demand for an item. They usually have thousands of items to promote, hundreds of locations to cover, and representatives who are short on time. Each salesperson can usually meet with any given retailer for only a few minutes.

The main difference between a wholesaler and a distributor is that wholesalers usually purchase, take delivery on, and warehouse merchandise themselves. Distributors often only have a sales force whose job is to take orders that are then forwarded to the manufacturer to ship. (There are some exceptions to this, however.)

SIX STEPS YOU CAN FOLLOW TO PICK THE RIGHT DISTRIBUTOR OR WHOLESALER

1. Be sure you understand what the organization will and won't do for you. Be sure you need their services in the first place.

2. Ask a few good retailers for their recommendations. Find out what your competition is doing in this area.

3. Shop around. Visit firms you're considering working with. Ask questions; these people probably know a great deal about your market.

4. Supply all the firms you "interview" with necessary materials: samples, price lists, catalogs, marketing plans, test results, and so on. Gauge the reactions and enthusiasm levels.

5. Be prepared to pay. Distributors and wholesalers can reach outlets you can't, and will expect somewhat higher discounts or larger slices of the pie than you offer other customers. Get the best deal you can, but don't bother working with an ineffective company just because the terms are good.

6. Check the mechanics. How long will your goods sit in someone's warehouse before they reach the customer? Will there be additional invoicing problems? What deadlines must be met?

"How can I design memorable business cards?"

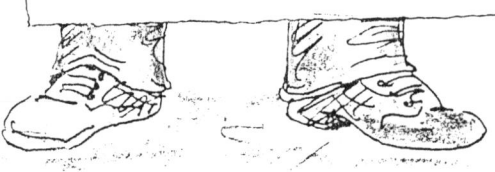

> People miss many opportunities in this area. And that's a shame. Business cards are so easy and inexpensive to produce that there's really no excuse for passing out boring ones.

So here's a suggestion you're strongly urged to follow. Take out your business card and look at it now. If it looks like a million others, with contact information and company name placed in a thoroughly predictable fashion, and no exciting graphic elements, throw all versions of that business card away and design new ones. What's it going to cost you to do so? More important, what is it costing you now to pass out boring advertisements no one will remember?

That, you see, is exactly what a business card is: an advertisement. And it carries more impact than many other types of advertisements. In many ways, a business card is a marketer's dream: an ad that people carry around with them and refer to later on!

> Compare your business card to those used by the top five or ten companies in town. They must be doing something right--and they may have had their cards professionally designed. Do you see any ideas you like?

You should test and rank your business cards as you would any other piece of promotional material. (See the section on testing with target groups elsewhere in this book.) It should compare well with cards used by successful companies. The card should also stand out immediately and convey a sense of what your company is and what kind of people stand behind it. Of course, it should feature all the necessary contact information in an easily legible format. Some of the better business cards out now are set in a vertical, rather than horizontal, format. This is an easy way to stand out from the crowd right away.

Another good idea is to use both sides of the card: one side for all the important contact information, and the other for a short message or special offer to customers. ("24-hour turnaround on all jobs!" "Present this card for a 10% discount on your first purchase!" "Ask us about our new Model X Widget!") There's very little extra cost involved--and people write on the back of the things all the time, anyway! Why not get their attention?

Today's consumer is increasingly fussy about product quality, applicability, and style. That fact makes life difficult for many of us who buy gifts for friends or loved ones. However, you can turn this situation to your advantage by mounting a low-budget gift certificate campaign.

And I do mean low-budget. All that's really required is a good-looking sign in your retail outlet (or a handsome "house ad" in your catalog). It might read something like this:

"LOOKING FOR A GIFT FOR THAT SPECIAL SOMEONE? Choose the present that's always right: a gift certificate from Widgetville. Available at any checkout counter in $10.00, $25.00, and $50.00 denominations. Buy one today!"

Such a gift is sure to please; after all, the recipient makes the choice!

There's so much variety available in the consumer goods area these days that the choices can be bewildering for many. Appeal to those buyers who are uncertain or confused about a gift purchase, and watch your sales rise!

Yes. And it represents an idea some businesses foolishly ignore. In a way, that's good, because it can allow you to short-circuit others in your field (who may have bigger budgets).

The strategy is to make it easy for the customer to buy from you. Our society is an increasingly fast-paced one. Our population is composed to a greater and greater degree of people who are short on time. Those businesses that expect purchasing patterns of fifteen, twenty, or twenty-five years ago to provide a firm basis for strategy into the next century are living in a dream world. Those that bend over backwards to make buying a product or service easy and convenient will have an advantage.

One of the key trends on the rise is to make your product or service available during times other than "standard business hours." You probably see this yourself in many areas. Most people's experience of what used to be known as "banker's hours," for instance, has been radically altered. The bank's hours, for all but the most complicated transactions, are dictated by the person whose account number is stamped on a personal ATM card. The very act of "shopping," which once, by definition, entailed a trip to a retail outlet of some sort, is now often associated with a catalog or home shopping broadcast, a toll-free 800 number, and next-day package delivery service. Even the national pastime has had to adjust to the needs of a population on the go. Ask the management of the Chicago Cubs, who opted to overturn a tradition that had endured for decades--by scheduling night games at Wrigley Field.

Growing, visionary businesses in the Nineties and beyond will: schedule retail hours of operation to take advantage of evening and weekend shoppers; obtain toll-free 800 lines and include the numbers in catalogs; keep an eye on advances in personal computer networks that will present new marketing opportunities; offer overnight delivery service as an option to their customers; and make inroads to workplace and "public area" markets.

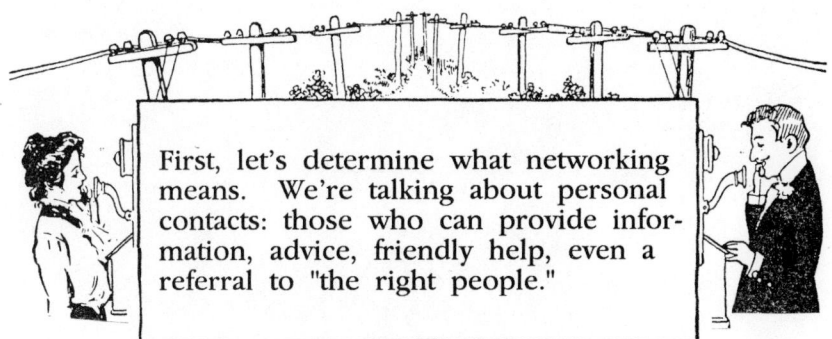

First, let's determine what networking means. We're talking about personal contacts: those who can provide information, advice, friendly help, even a referral to "the right people."

Personal contacts, as most people know, can make a great deal of difference in a career, in marketing work, and in business at all levels. It's a fact of life--contracts often go to friends. Sometimes (not always) WHO you know really can be just as important as WHAT you know.

How can you make networking work for you? Talk, meet, visit, and work with people. Develop and "collect" personal contacts--as one would gems. Join clubs and social organizations, especially those frequented by business people of interest to you. Become active in a cause; take an interest in issues facing your community. Just as important--show respect, appreciation, need, and liking for people. It's not enough to develop an interest; develop a sincere interest. Try to help your contacts, not simply look for ways to take advantage of them. Blatant offers of reciprocal "back-scratching" will backfire. Instead, make an effort to, say, steer customers toward acquaintances if you can. Promptly oblige them if they make a request of you. Don't worry about what people owe you; the advantage you seek will usually develop in short order, without heavy handed posturing on your part.

Don't fall out of touch. Maintain constant contact, even if only by the occasional postcard or phone call. Do this with those who might end up to be a big help to you, but with others as well. "Unimportant" contacts can surprise you. Go out on a limb for people, and they'll usually try to do the same for you. Contrary to what you may have heard, networking is rarely free. However, it does frequently have a low cost in comparison with its benefits.

When should you use networking? When you see problems or opportunities. When you find there are network resources available to you that might help you get your job done. When you're not afraid to extend a little time, effort, and humility. The result in the best cases is a pleasant one: everybody gains, both personally and professionally! (And you build real, live, reciprocal friendships too, which doesn't hurt.)

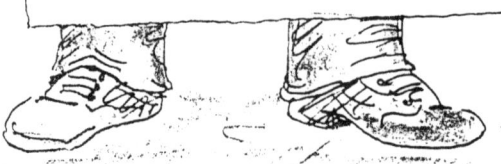

The best idea here is probably to attend industry and trade shows related to your business.

Think about it. You spend lots of time, effort, and money trying to get your message in front of a certain target audience (say, building contractors). Perhaps you have purchased a qualified mailing list, initiated a telemarketing program, or even taken out paid display advertising. All for what?

To reach a certain group of people--indirectly! You can do exactly the same thing at trade shows and industry-related events ... on a person-to-person basis.

You might decide, for instance, to attend one of the many "home shows" that are held in virtually every major metropolitan area of the country. Such an event is likely to be heavily attended by important industry contacts--and quite a few potential customers! The costs are usually minimal. And the "networking" potential is enormous.

Whether the group you want to reach is industry "insiders" or highly qualified customers, you're likely to find both groups represented in abundance at the key trade shows, conventions, and industry functions related to your business. Take the time to participate by securing a good booth location and assembling a professional display. You'll find it's well worth your effort.

You may have little choice. If your market facts tell you that all your competitors are selling widgets at one dollar, and if one dollar is the absolute least you can charge and still survive, then the decision makes itself. This, however, is rare; you usually have some flexibility.

Your price (less costs) sets your income-- at least on that one sale. Very few businesses, of course, can survive on just one sale. So your income, in actuality, is based on your price, multiplied by your number of units of sale, minus your costs.

Your price influences your customers. Some customers buy on price alone, or with price as a key factor. A very few ignore price completely. Most seek the greatest value, real or imagined, per dollar. (This factor is usually known as "perceived value.")

The "ceiling" and the "floor" are terms that describe the highest and lowest possible price decisions you can make. Your ceiling might be what your competition is offering; your floor might be the lowest price you can charge and still turn a profit.

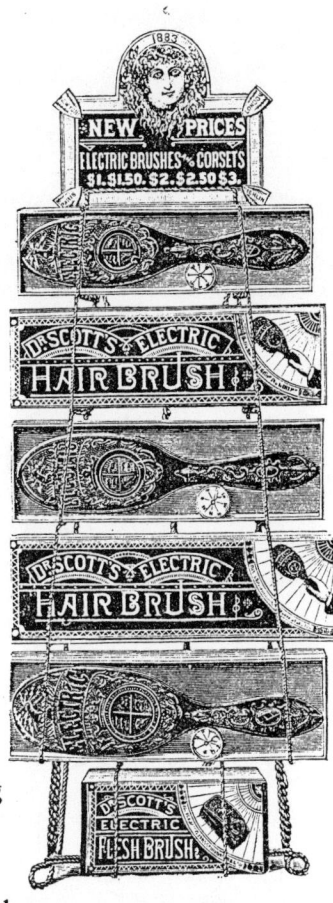

Sometimes, you may wish, briefly, to sell below your cost, in order to get customers to try your product or service. Eventually, of course, you must sell above your cost in order to build gross profit--that is, the dollars that allow you to keep your business in operation.

If you are more efficient than your competitor, you might sell below their price and still generate enough income to pay all your other costs (like salaries and rent) and still end up with a net (or bottom line) profit. If you do sell below your competitor's price, you'll probably aim to sell enough extra units to make up for the lost income from lower price. Your gross will very likely be lower than the competitor's on each individual sale. By the same token, higher real or perceived value can let you sell above your competition's price. This can cut your number of units sold (just as a lower price raised them). However, if you can compensate for the reduction by the extra dollars you'll see with a higher price, income goes up.

151

Pricing should be a window, not a barrier. For instance, volume discounts to key larger customers usually increase your efficiency and profitability, and thus represent a reasonable basis for a price reduction.

Clearly, your decision can be a little tricky. Your price should probably be somewhere between your cost and your competitor's price. If you decide to charge more than a competitor, you'd better have some impressive marketing strategies and/or a superior product or service.

NINE TIPS ON EFFECTIVE PRICING STRATEGY

1) More products fail because of a price that's too low than because of a price that's too high.

2) It's easier to cut prices than raise them.

3) "Prestige" pricing can often build your perceived value.

4) One particularly effective strategy is to start out with a relatively high "prestige" price, then cut the price later. The result is a high perceived level of quality, plus a "value" look.

5) A low (or "defensive") price can discourage new competitors.

6) Price testing with a sample group of consumers is an excellent way to get important information. Check for positive or negative reactions at various price levels.

7) Price in such a way that you build up your bottom line.

8) Don't get involved in price conspiracy or rigging agreements.

9) Remember: your pricing strategy should attract customers and confuse competitors.

Price is a vitally important element in your market strategy. You can usually change it rapidly, unlike your product or its packaging. With effective, intelligent pricing, you can out-maneuver, out-market, and out-sell your competitor . . . and get a bigger share of the market.

The reunion of business-school alumni was going well. In the corner, over drinks from the open bar, two old friends were discussing times gone by. "What do you think happened to Myron Lavolt?" one asked. "You mean Myron Dimbulb?" the other responded. "You mean the dumbest guy in the class of 1979?"

A professor who'd had the two in her elementary accounting class overheard the conversation. "I happen to know," she said, "that Myron Lavolt is now the president of his own retail chain. He employs 1500 people. He earns a salary of a little over five and a half million dollars a year, and his business is going nowhere but up. And what's more, you two are absolutely right. I have to admit that he was without doubt the least promising student I ever worked with. Frankly, I'm mystified. I don't know how he did it." The two alumni stared at her in disbelief.

Just then, through the window, they saw a huge stretch limousine pull up to the hotel. The driver got out, went around to the side of the car, and opened the door. Out stepped Myron Lavolt: immaculately dressed, smiling, sporting expensive jewelry and a gold-handled walking stick. A trio of bodyguards accompanied him into the reception hall.

He was the star of the reunion. People clustered all around him, hoping that whatever luck he'd encountered would rub off on them. Finally, at the end of the evening, the professor's curiosity got the better of her. She walked up to Myron Lavolt and looked him in the eye. "Myron," she said. "Tell me. Tell me how you did it. What on earth did you do to turn things around?"

"Well," he answered, "I follow one simple rule. I make sure I charge prices at a three percent markup. That's the secret."

"Three percent? That's all?" The professor was dumbfounded.

"Yep," replied Myron. "That's it. Three percent. If something costs me a dollar, I price it at three dollars."

WINNING THE BATTLE BEFORE YOU GO TO WAR: MARKETING STRATEGY AND TACTICS FOR YOUR BUSINESS

This is a common problem. In many markets and product/service categories, one or two dominant companies make life extremely difficult for the other players. They capture (or steal) larger and larger slices of the pie. In some cases, they put the smaller firms out of business entirely. Occasionally, this is deliberate strategy employed with some ruthlessness. The logic: It is easier to push a weak brand out of the market 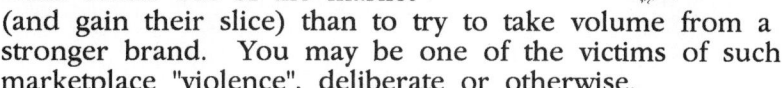 (and gain their slice) than to try to take volume from a stronger brand. You may be one of the victims of such marketplace "violence", deliberate or otherwise.

"Pay attention to your competitors," said the Old Marketing Sage, "for they are the first to discover your errors." In a way, the pressure you're receiving is a very good sign; it's pointing up your vulnerabilities. Often, you can build up or defend your weak spots before events reach crisis proportions.

HERE ARE SOME POSSIBLE STEPS.

1) First, study the market action carefully. List exactly what the competition is doing. When? Where? How?

2) Now ask, "Are there any of these steps I could also take, or even improve upon?" Sometimes your market "intelligence" (for instance salespeople, dealers, or friends) may discover a competitor's plan, allowing you to announce a better one . . . two weeks ahead of the competition.

3) Always remember that the other guys are out to gain a larger piece of the market pie. They could be (and probably are) after YOUR slice! Don't sit passively and watch it happen.

4) Beat them to the punch. Sometimes even a slight move on your part can negate, offset or even eliminate the opposition's program. For example, if they offer a discount of X% you might offer the same, plus Y% more. If they offer a new product, you may be able to unveil two, each of which features several product improvements and customer benefits. Sometimes you can't afford to exceed or even match the steps. However, you might APPEAR to be doing so by making a richer offer . . . but only for a very short time.

5) Raise (do NOT lower) the quality level. Improve the product, its package design, size, display, or distribution. Think long and hard before you jeopardize your hard-won reputation with your customers. It is one of your most important assets.

6) Listen to the grapevine. Find out how other smaller companies are meeting the challenges you're facing. You may be able to take advantage of someone else's brilliant idea.

Fortunately, you can beat your competition by working smarter, not harder. One way is to improve your advertising (if you're using any, that is). Find a better theme that uses the same ad media budget; good ads and poor ads cost the same to run. (See the Table of Contents for references to some ideas on how to run successful advertising campaigns.)

Case history: Royal Crown Cola, Ltd. (Canada) was the "new kid on the block," a recent entrant to a huge market. Entrenched brands like Coke and Pepsi intended to stay that way.

Astute Canadian management (i.e., the author) studied successful steps used by U.S. bottlers and applied their techniques in Canada. Account opener deals were offered, and arrangements for special displays made. New ads (previously tested) were launched.

Royal Crown salespeople learned of actions planned by their giant competitors: five-cents-off coupons on a six-pack. The "little guy" hit the market earlier with a ten-cents-off program, loaded retailers with special product, and fought for shelf space so little remained when the larger firms came in with their offer. Shortly thereafter, Royal Crown launched a major contest promotion, which delivered positive results.

> The market leaders may be giants, but giants usually cannot move as fast as their smaller rivals. Your size can be your secret weapon, and the best way to keep the competition from killing you in the market.

Many firms find it quite difficult to make top-notch marketing efforts in the face of major business challenges. Such challenges might include: entrenched competition; sudden doses of bad publicity for your firm; major shifts in consumer tastes or attitudes; a declining national economy; or difficulty matching the quality and/or resources of others in your market. You may even confront all of the above simultaneously.

Nobody promised it was going to be easy. Try to keep your head above water, and make a mental note not to overreact to problems.

Get the facts. Study them carefully; be sure you're not acting on third-hand reports or emotionally charged interpretations. Then--study. As we learned earlier, a problem well defined is usually half solved.

Look at your resources. What unique strengths or aptitudes can you or your firm bring to bear? What, for that matter, are your competitors doing? Could you consider their approach? Remember that there are many firms whose answer to a difficult business environment might be more marketing, not less.

If you determine that belt-tightening is in order, and you want to cut your marketing costs, don't just slash away without thinking. Make the decisions carefully, and realize that there are usually going to be some consequences. There are very few "painless" choices in this area; however, the following ideas represent a good starting point for maximizing your precious marketing resources (read: dollars) in a harsh environment.

Step One: Simplify your research work. For many companies, informal polling or one-on-one conversation with consumers will yield results equivalent to those obtained through more sophisticated methods.

Step Two: Streamline your production efforts. Many firms find that if they cut down on freelance or agency design costs, for instance, the resulting "plain" advertisements may actually carry more impact! Be sure to consult the Million Dollar Checklist, as well as the other guidelines on advertising and promotional pieces, found elsewhere in this book.

Step Three: Jettison unprofitable endeavors--and keep your eyes open for new opportunities. It may be a cliche, but it really is a very ill wind that blows no one good. This might be the time to close down marginal operations. And in a bad economy, you may be able to obtain a promising new product or service line from a faltering company--and market it to your advantage!

Of course, all this should be done in concert with company-wide efforts to build teamwork, control costs, heighten margins, and deliver verifiable "pay-back" every step of the way. During very tough times, the best overall approach is probably to level with key colleagues and employees, build a group approach, and inspire excellence. All that, plus someone with a clear head at the top of the organization, may well see you through.

A sense of humor doesn't hurt, either. Now, more than ever, you need some perspective. Try to enjoy yourself, even when you're confronted by obstacles.

"We're doing great! Any suggestions on how best to market during the good times?"

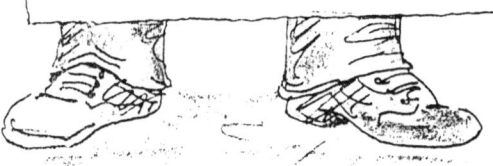

Don't rest on your laurels. Whatever you've done to get yourself to this level of success, it probably involved no small measures of brains and hustle. Don't let yourself go soft now--when you can consolidate your gains, and perhaps even soar higher!

The goal is still to grow . . . but you can now go about achieving growth in different ways. Put your resources to work so you can strengthen your position, and perhaps even get out in front of a couple of your competitors. Profitability must be your keystone, no matter how big you get. Remember the old saying: "In times of peace, prepare for war."

Take a few more risks than you might have a couple of years back--but don't go overboard. (People can go broke even in the best of times.) Was there some project you once thought about seriously, but rejected because you couldn't afford to do anything other than to think conservatively? Maybe now is the time to re-examine that project.

Develop an opportunistic mindset. You'll probably notice new, potentially profitable marketing concepts all around you, waiting to be fleshed out. Perhaps these are ideas you simply couldn't pursue when your main goal was keeping the business going from one day to the next. You now have the time to stop and thoroughly evaluate a good, original initiative.

Follow through; complete your projects. Good times present so many opportunities that some people are tempted to jump from one project to another, completing virtually nothing. That's a good way to lose the ground you've worked so hard to win. Don't let it happen.

Smile! These are fun times.

Assembling your marketing budget is the natural, rational response to the inevitable questions, "Hey--how much is this going to cost me, anyway? And what am I going to get in return?"

If income is important to you (as it is to most of us), then you should take the time to put together a realistic budget. When it comes to allocating your company's precious resources, balance is everything. Too small an investment may doom your project. Too much optimism can cause unacceptable losses.

Your early marketing "costs" are likely to be time, thought, planning, and revision. These things do take time, and if they take time, they eat up cash. But it's almost always money well spent. Later, major marketing costs can include any number of things: commissions for salespeople, printing, media, and so on. However, if you plan correctly, these expenditures will actually work as investments, rather than costs--because they can repay you handsomely.

Keep a simple P&L statement in mind. Your sales may equal $1,000. The cost of producing your goods or providing your service may equal $600. That leaves $400, out of which must come all other costs, including your income, tax, overhead expenses, and--last, but EMPHATICALLY not least--marketing costs. Put it all together, and you have a simple, compelling argument. Spend less than $400, and you'll show a loss.

Now go one step further--work out your projections on paper. Define each item, whether expenditure or income, in terms of its relationship to sales (expressed as a percentage). Here's an example.

ITEM	AMOUNT	% OF SALES
Income:		
Actual revenue from sales	$1000	100%
==		
TOTAL INCOME	$1000	100%
Costs:		
Manufacturing	$600	60%
Salaries	$100	10%
Tax	$50	5%
Marketing	$200	20%
TOTAL COSTS	$950	95%
PROFIT	$50	5%

... a Marketing Budget

You can see why it's so important to a) streamline your operation so that it's as efficient as possible in producing revenue; and b) keep your costs down to the lowest levels you can.

Taken together, these two objectives increase your profitability. It's in putting together your budgets that you'll specify exactly how you plan to accomplish these twin goals.

THE WINNING BUDGET PLANNER USUALLY . . .

   . . . invests enough to do the job.

   . . . invests carefully and wisely.

   . . . makes sure every dollar is working its hardest.

   . . . institutes careful cost control measures.

   . . . considers and reconsiders every single expense, even (especially!) the small ones, which, cumulatively, can "nickel-and-dime" you to death.

Typical marketing budget items would include fact gathering and interviewing (usually an investment of your time rather than ready cash); printing and brochures; packaging (though this often ends up under "manufacturing"; you'll have to develop your own guidelines); sales commissions; media and advertising... and many more. You may not want to (or be able to) budget for each of these items yet. But you should know WHAT you are spending, and you should make your decisions based on something more than a momentary whim.

Assume you're going to get ruthless about your budgets. You decide to cut, from the example above, the $200 of "fat" you think you see in the marketing department. Well--common sense would seem to tell you that your profit is going to go from $50 to $250. Right?

Usually, the answer is a very loud "wrong." Here's how the project might actually turn out if you eliminate your marketing efforts:

ITEM	AMOUNT	% OF SALES
Income:		
Actual revenue from sales	$750	100%
===		
TOTAL INCOME	$750	100%
Costs:		
Manufacturing	$600	80%
Salaries	$100	13%
Tax	$50	7%
Marketing	$0	0%
TOTAL COSTS	$750	100%
PROFIT	$0	0%

Good marketing builds sales momentum, which in turn builds profitability. Initially (say, during the first few months of a product launch), you are investing. Your sales may be little or nothing. But as the program takes hold and generates sales, you will (you hope) build up revenues.

Again, there are no guarantees . . . but a good, solid budget will help you accurately identify the risks, as well as those crucial break-even points. That way, you'll know what you're up against.

"Can a small company like mine implement successful marketing ideas from the Japanese?"

Some of the most successful marketing people in Japan study intensely the 400-year-old code followed by the samurai warriors--and follow that code religiously.

The code is demanding, but can be adapted to Western marketing efforts with great success. The most important strategic steps, usually followed quite aggressively in the Land of the Rising Sun, are summarized below.

1) Learn many arts. It will be difficult, but constant study will increase your abilities. Don't inflate your self-image; expand your base of skills. Know yourself. Think about your goals. Strive constantly for self-improvement.

2) Know your team's abilities if you plan to lead. Work in small groups, and assign tasks based on demonstrated strengths. Watch the results; stay in circulation, so that you can anticipate problems before they develop.

3) Maintain your resources wisely; reject wasteful activity. Your "weapons" must be without defect and immediately accessible. Your actions should be efficient, precise, and goal-oriented at all times. Do nothing that has no use.

4) Use your resources to the fullest. Do not rely on one "weapon" exclusively; make use of every tool and every advantage you have.

5) Demand victory from yourself. Your objective is not to make it through the day, not to get by, but to excel. Consider each day a "battle" against inefficiency, mediocrity, and inattention to customer needs and desires.

6) Take advantage of situations as they develop. Cultivate judgment and resolve; remember that timing can be everything. Be cunning, determined, and calm. When you act, act after due consideration--and decisively.

7) Avoid falling victim to deception. Listen, but do not rule out the possibility that your information may not be sound.

8) Do not repeat errors. Win with correct strategy, not brute strength; formulate a sound plan of attack.

9) In confronting an opponent (that is, a competitor): stay erect and watchful; learn what "weapons" the enemy uses; attack when an opening presents itself; watch for opportunities to spread anger, fear, and confusion on the other side; when you have an advantage, press it to its utmost. Attempt to destroy your adversary utterly.

The Japanese, it is estimated, are seven times more productive than we are. Not just 100%, mind you, but 700% more productive per capita. It's a sobering statistic, but it's something to keep in mind the next time you hear people complaining about "unfair competition." One of the main techniques the Japanese use "unfairly" against us is to work much, much harder than we do.

Smaller firms in this country, however, are in an excellent position to adapt the ideas that make such productivity explosions possible. Marketing is a particularly good place to start, because it can have an immediate impact on your company's success.

"Quality circles" require regular team meetings. Each member must recommend some improvement in the product, service, or system in question. This approach can yield dramatic positive results.

Typical watchwords of successful Japanese marketing strategies include: consensus; futurism; quality control; innovation; imitation; and competitive spirit.

Typical attitudes of successful Japanese managers include: thoroughness; resourcefulness; progressive thinking; discipline; dedication; precision; organization; respect for all team members; and commitment to open lines of communication.

Japanese managers, in marketing or just about any other field, tend to: leave people room to save face; acknowledge that they have not learned everything; motivate team members in group discussions; build mutual trust; and offer tangible examples of a strong work ethic by putting in long hours, working hard, and accepting personal responsibility for the group's results.

PERSON-TO-PERSON: IDEAS OF SPECIAL INTEREST TO RETAILERS, RESTAURANT OPERATORS, AND OTHER "PEOPLE" FIELDS

"I run a small retail operation. How can I win customers from the big guys?"

Answer: Out-maneuver them and make their ideas work for you. Retailing is perhaps the most visible business field of them all. However, good retail marketing is not easy, and even the dominant companies have been known to drop the ball now and then.

Here are some guidelines that have been proven in action--following them will help you make the most of your opportunities.

1) Be ruthless in evaluating your location. If it's not what you need, or if it's providing a mediocre sales environment, move somewhere else (a tactic slow-moving companies can't always follow expeditiously). It's a commonplace in retailing that location is perhaps the single most important factor at your disposal. Find a location that meets your objectives (including, of course, affordability) and make the most of the traffic flow there.

2) Cultivate a positive company atmosphere. You know how annoying it is to have to deal with a clerk at a department store who's incompetent, rude, ill-trained, or a combination of all three. Your employees needn't (can't!) project such an image to customers. Fortunately, because you're small enough to make pride in your organization a hands-on reality, your staff can win points for politeness and helpfulness. Remember: part of the "product" in any retail organization is the human factor. Make it work for you. (Lots of big companies don't make it work for them!)

3) Arrange your floor plan for high sales levels. That's what the big chains do: impulse items and high-markup goods up front, near the checkout position; "shopping" items in the back. Other proven winners at floor-level: point-of-purchase displays at shoulder level; brochures outlining benefits of big-ticket items; and "shelf-talkers"-- essentially, promotional pieces designed for placement in the aisles themselves.

4) If appropriate, offer in-store test samples. A good percentage of those who try will purchase the product, and the technique often costs virtually nothing!

5) Finally, know your market. What does your "average" customer like? Dislike? Consider expensive? How does he or she react to "special sales"? On an in-person level, you can often obtain such crucial information (through interviews, questionnaires, or good old informal conversation), act on it, and reap the benefits--all before your big-time competition finishes the internal proposal necessary to authorize a market research effort.

"If I'm in retail, I don't have to worry about packaging, do I?"

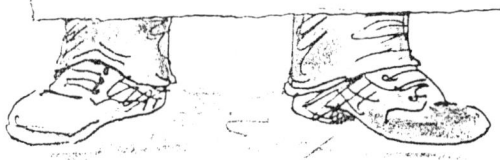

Wrong! Your "package" is your store. If it's run-down or unattractive, you might as well close up shop.

If your business is traffic-sensitive, be sure you are working in a good location for both walk-in pedestrian access and auto traffic. Be sure your facility's exterior says, "Welcome . . . come in!"

Once the customer makes it into your building, make sure he or she will feel good about what's there--and want to do business.

Finally, compare your location, exterior, and interior to those of your top competitors. Yours has to be at least as good, perhaps better.

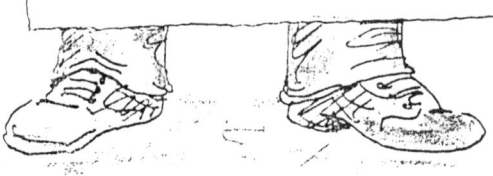

"Will I sell more if my inventory is large and varied?"

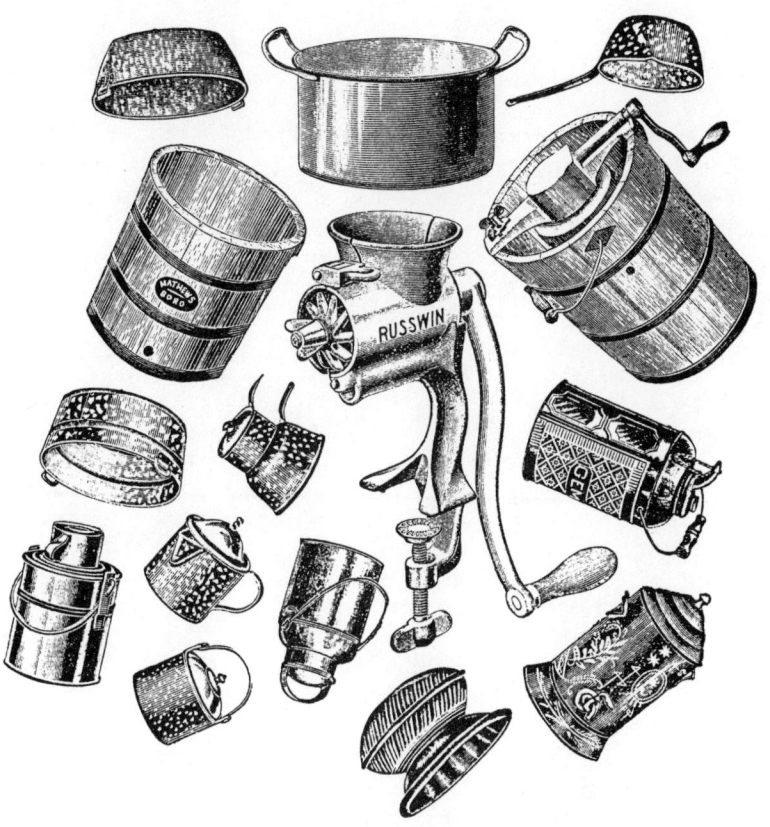

The answer, unfortunately, is one of those annoying "yes-and-no" varieties. Yes, if your customers are accustomed to choosing from a wide selection and receiving their choice right away. No, if the customer group requires only a few major items, and doesn't mind waiting for (or not receiving at all) the less popular items.

With this question, we have come to the much-discussed topic of "niche-dom."

A major department store builds much of its sales volume on the appeal of an extensive inventory. Typically, this features a wide variety of gadgets, attachments, and cutting-edge products. A corner convenience store's profits, in contrast, depend far less on variety. That store's success is founded on the idea that you can run in at midnight and buy a box of cornflakes, even though the store does not have all brands of cereal.

Inventory is a two-edged sword. On the one hand, you must have at least a reasonable selection of goods or services, or your customers will go elsewhere. On the other hand, inventory can be quite expensive, and you must be certain that your investments in it are wise ones.

If you buy a new car outright, you'll spend, say, $12,000 in ready cash. You could have placed that $12,000 in the bank and earned significant interest over the course of one year. Instead of saving the money, however, you decided to buy the car. Now, this probably doesn't make a lot of difference to you if you drive the car every day. If, however, the car is delivered, and you never drive it for the whole year, the fact is you have essentially thrown away the money you could have earned at the bank. And for what? For the privilege of looking at the car that's sitting there in your garage.

Much of your inventory is in fact just going to sit in your garage (or warehouse). Maybe not for a whole year . . . but, then again, you never know. And we haven't even begun to talk about the cost of your space, light, heat, and the other costs you'll incur in storing the merchandise.

So: inventory is expensive. The best approach is probably to keep it at the minimum level necessary to do the job and fill your orders.

Beware of over-purchasing. It's tempting. Salespeople can be persuasive. They may have special prices to induce you to buy larger amounts. Still, you must be careful. Many people forget about the costs involved and income lost in storing inventory, but your "stock on hand" does represent a decision to tie up capital. Could that money be put to more profitable use elsewhere in your business?

The best advice on large purchasing (with its attendant price breaks) is to wait until your business is well established. At that point, your inventory needs and use patterns will be known, and you'll probably even be able to make accurate volume estimates on sales programs.

Have a "re-order point" on each item. This should take into account the delivery time required to restock. Let's say it takes two weeks for you to receive an order of widgets. You should order no later than the point at which you reach a two-week supply. Remember: "out-of-stock" positions represent lost opportunity. Large corporations have the whole process automated; every item is keyed through a computerized code. When supplies reach a certain level, a reorder goes out automatically. You may have to do a little educated guessing, but the general pattern is still good to follow.

To minimize the pain of keeping inventory, see how much flexibility your suppliers have. Some will supply low interest rates on big-ticket items; others will allow "long dating" on an invoice. This allows you, for instance, to pay in 120 days rather than 30.

And now, a joke from the marketing humor hall of fame. A traveler walked into a small grocery store, and, after looking around, said to the owner, "You sure have a nice store here. I can't help noticing, though, that the whole back wall is stacked to the ceiling with packages of salt. You certainly must sell a lot of salt in this part of the country!"

The owner looked at the huge barricade of salt, scratched his head, and said, "Well, no. I don't really sell that much salt. But the salt salesman sells a lot of salt."

... a Marketing Budget   **191**

Marketing savvy can often determine which restaurants will succeed and which will fail. Yet most restaurants (that is to say, most of your competitors) are not in a position to take advantage of all that solid, smart, inexpensive marketing efforts have to offer.

HERE ARE TEN IDEAS
THAT WIN CUSTOMERS
AND VISIBILITY:

1) Local publicity can work to your advantage if you offer press releases outlining strong stories of human interest, your restaurant's history, or interesting facts about your clientele. Many restaurants forget the most basic step of all: inviting the food critics! (Of course, when such people do arrive at your door, make sure they receive your usual excellent service.)

2) Location is every bit as crucial to your business as it is to a retailer; make sure you're getting your fair share of the foot traffic. If you're not, move. Once you do find the right spot, be sure to feature your menu and any positive reviews right out front, where everyone can see them. Is the facility safe? Easy to get to? Does it provide sufficient parking? Is it clearly visible at night?

3) In-house premiums can pay off handsomely. "Enjoy a steak and your dessert comes free!" This can build up profitability by winning more orders for higher-priced items.

4) Weekly promotions can increase your customer base. Examples for a family restaurant might include free meals for kids on Wednesdays, or a ragtime piano player every Tuesday night. Display these on your marquee or sidewalk display unit. (Many successful restaurants offer DAILY promotions!)

5) Emphasis on personal selling is key. Did someone call that employee of yours a waiter? He's not a waiter! He's a salesperson! As such, he must have tact, charisma, enthusiasm, and high levels of self-confidence and motivation. Your waiters and waitresses are your conduit to customers, and they must be selected, trained, supervised, and paid accordingly. If they think they're in a dead-end job . . . you operate a dead-end restaurant!

6) Getting on the floor and talking to the customers is recommended procedure for restaurant managers. It shows individual attention to the customer and provides you with important facts. If you're above and beyond "management by walking around," you're likely to be cut out of the communication cycle. Not a good idea. Never be intrusive, but do invite comments tactfully and professionally. Ask--in person--how the customers feel about your service. Ask--in person--what you can do to make things better. Ask--in person--whether the food meets expectations.

7) Reaction to customer input is particularly important in the restaurant business. This is because of the importance of repeat business and the general immediacy of the environment. People who are frustrated at a bank's accounting error may overlook it in the future; people who are mistreated at a restaurant tend never to return again. Do more than just avoid "scenes"-- actively solicit your customers (perhaps through questionnaires) for ways you can improve. And remember: an angry customer is almost always telling you something you need to hear.

8) Advertising? If so, check your competition carefully. You may want to build on existing awareness by publicizing special menu days or offering price-off coupons. You may simply want to imitate what works for others . . . but be sure to check it against the Million Dollar Checklist, found elsewhere in this book.

9) The best promotional work in the world can't help a restaurant that's dingy, dirty, or generally unappetizing. Make sure the "package" you present to the consumer is one he or she will want to see more of.

10) If it's broke, fix it. You may want to consider a complete rethinking of the basic idea that is your restaurant. Would you be better off as a lunch spot than as a dinner spot? Offering gourmet dining rather than family fare? Switching to a 24-hour schedule? Research extensively, and look before you leap; but if a change is in order, make it.

Whatever approach you decide on, it should be one that conserves your capital and wrings every last drop of effectiveness out of your efforts. For small businesses, the watchword is caution. For most startup home-based businesses (should we call them "micro-businesses"?) the rule is even more important: don't invest a dime until you're absolutely positive about the results you'll be likely to receive.

Say your brother-in-law has a great idea about advertising, and can get you a "special deal" for a mere "X" dollars; think twice. If it doesn't work out, who's going to be the one to write the check for the bad ad space? You--or your brother-in-law?

Concentrate on the very safest bets: those efforts that can heighten your profile among likely customers for minimal dollars. These would include high-quality business cards, stationery, and lists of former clients. Other "low-/no-budget" items that have proven effective for home-based businesses: notices in local media outlets such as church and community newsletters; press releases announcing the business to smaller newspapers for whom such an event may be newsworthy; and "word-of-mouth" campaigns among your friends and associates.

It costs a little money, but many small businesses, nevertheless, decide to take out a good-looking ad in the local Yellow Pages. Doing so can heighten your visibility, reinforce your professional image, and generates inquiries. Bear in mind, though, that for many businesses, the Yellow Pages represent a potential waste of money rather than a real opportunity. (The topic is addressed in more detail elsewhere in this book.)

Try to identify a discrete portion of the public that is likely to use your product or service, then choose the most cost-effective way to reach that group. Avoid scattershot mailings and advertisements at this stage. The odds are, you're more likely to convince a few people of your superior work (and it must be superior!) than all the potential customers in a huge metropolitan area. In the early going, the name of the game will be finding and keeping customers. And quality is the key. Remember that, in virtually all environments, you must be significantly better than the competition if you hope to gain entry into the market in any meaningful way.

The vast majority of home-based-businesses fail within the first year. That might be sobering news, but then again, most such businesses don't take huge financial risks, either. The losses you may encounter if things don't work out can be minimized. Don't go overboard on any one idea, especially if you haven't tested it. Once you achieve the important goal of still being in business after a few months, secure in your march toward profitability, you may well be in a position to implement some of the more elaborate (and potentially more profitable) ideas in this book.

Usually not, but the answer varies from business to business. This question is more difficult to answer than it once was, in part because many regions now offer two or more phone directories featuring paid display advertisements. Competition can drive ad rates down, and certain businesses are well advised to take advantage of a good deal in this area.

More important, there is a long-overdue trend toward making things as convenient as possible for the customer, and the argument can be made that a central resource such as the phone directory is a good place to start. Nevertheless, for many companies, the yellow pages are not the place to advertise.

Of course, you can't expect every call that comes to you as a result of the ad to be a sale. There are two main classes of responses: calls to get more information, and calls to place orders. Each is important, but you should bear the distinction in mind when evaluating any ad's effectiveness.

The only hard and fast rule in this area is that you must think like a customer. If your average prospect is likely to come to a decision to buy your product or service through consulting the phone directory, you should strongly consider some sort of display ad. Many businesses, however, do not fall into this category.

Think about your own use of the directory. The odds are that, when you need a locksmith, you reach for the phonebook. The same cannot be said of your selection of a video rental store, which, because of the large number of such businesses, is much more likely to based on the proximity of a given store to your home.

What kind of customers do you want to reach? What services do you offer them? Are they likely to phone you as the result of a sudden, unforeseen development? Finally, are your competitors advertising in the phone directory? If so, that argues in favor of similar exposure for your firm. If not, you may want to consider saving your money.

It's worth noting, while we're on the subject, that important technological advances have recently been made that may redefine the way we think of the phone directory. In France, a new system was recently installed that allowed people to hook their phone line directly to the personal computer in their home or office--and tap into a network of local merchants and service businesses! The system allows users to peruse catalogs, prices, product images, and even features question-and-answer sessions. Orders can be placed directly from the user's keyboard. In the United States, USWest is initiating a similar service, though as of this writing it has yet to expand nationally.

TO ADVERTISE OR NOT TO ADVERTISE

Our culture abounds with commercials. On television, on radio, on seemingly any and every flat surface potential customers are likely to see, you'll find an ad. Therefore, it seems, if you want to sell something, the first thing you should do is buy an ad of some sort. Or should you?

It's understandable that many small- and medium-sized operators begin their marketing plans with this question. Paid advertising represents that part of marketing to which people are exposed most often. However, it's usually not the best place to begin. And you certainly shouldn't begin (as many do) by leaping ahead to the question, "What's the best media buy for me?"

The best advice for many small businesses is to pick no media at all. Advertising is expensive, risky, and unforgiving; it's not for everyone. However, your field may require some large-scale consumer awareness campaign that does not fall into the "zero-dollar" categories covered elsewhere in this book.

If this is the case, and if, after due consideration, you decide that you should advertise, you should keep a number of factors in mind. They're outlined on the following pages. However . . .

If you're in any doubt, research the particulars of your situation thoroughly before committing any resources to advertising. The best advice is probably to contact your local SCORE (Service Corps of Retired Executives) or Small Business Administration representative for free advice.

"If I decide to advertise, how can I pick cost-effective media that will do the job?"

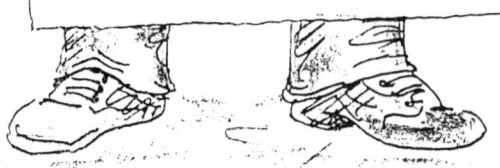

Don't place too much faith in the media salespeople. As sales reps battle for your dollars, you'll hear representatives of each format claiming to be the best by far for your needs. They can't all be right. Talk with a trusted colleague or professional contact about your specific requirements.

The secret to selecting media is to find a format that reaches your prospects with minimum waste and maximum clout. The actual method you select is simply the most efficient "container" for your selling message. Determining the various levels of efficiency--and getting the most bang for your media dollar--is usually a matter of:

1) Accurate forecasting of all costs (including production).

2) Preparing a good media plan. It needn't be more than a page long. The plan should include prospect counts, selling themes, goals, deadlines, schedules, and a brief assessment of the strengths and weaknesses of the two or three leading media candidates under consideration.

3) Following your gut instincts IN CONJUNCTION WITH what the numbers tell you.

Questions you should ASK about any given medium include:

What is this medium's reach/audience/readership/circulation?

Does this medium fit the themes I want to express about my products or services?

Who are my prospects?

Does this medium reach them?

What percentage of my target group will hear this message?

What percentage of the total audience of this medium is a member of my target group?

(Sales reps may be a little vague on these last two points. Don't let them get away with it. If they say they have no figures, ask them to make an informed estimate. If they say they can't, tell them you can't do business until they can.)

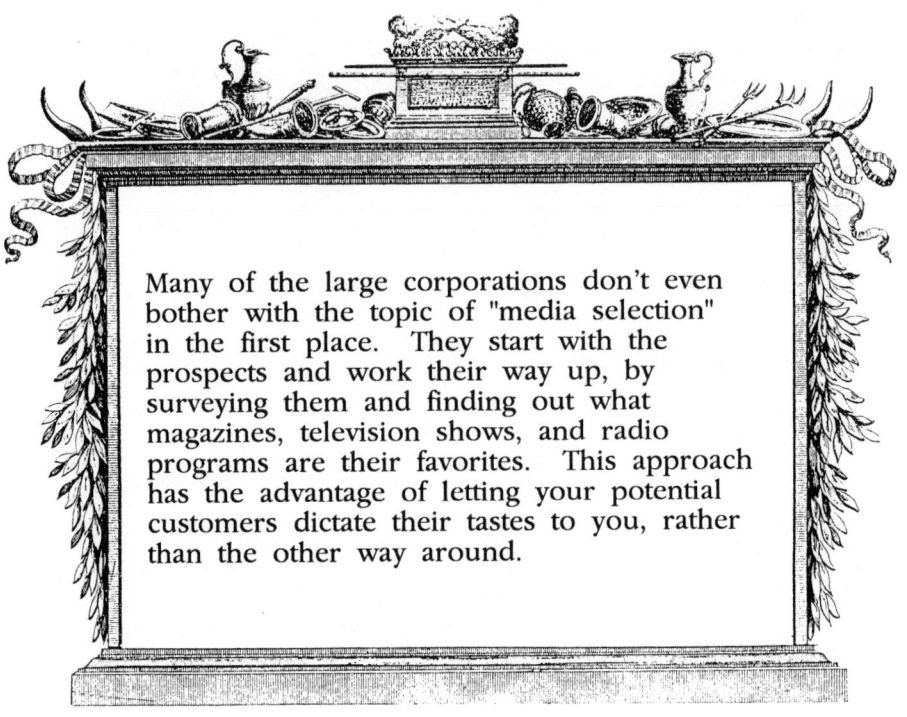

Many of the large corporations don't even bother with the topic of "media selection" in the first place. They start with the prospects and work their way up, by surveying them and finding out what magazines, television shows, and radio programs are their favorites. This approach has the advantage of letting your potential customers dictate their tastes to you, rather than the other way around.

Let's say, to use a hypothetical case, that "The Cosby Show" is the most popular television show in the country. You're considering taking out a prime time ad for your widgets during that program.

You've determined that your target group of potential customers consists exclusively of men and women under five feet tall who wear mismatched argyle socks--an infinitesimal portion of the general public. You do an informal survey of 125 such prospects. You discover, to your amazement, that while forty percent of the rest of the country watches "The Cosby Show" on any given Thursday night, less than one percent of your target group does so. Conclusion: Even though you'd be reaching many, many people by placing that prime time spot, ninety-nine percent plus of them are almost certainly going to have no interest in your widgets. "Cosby" is probably not a good media investment for you. (The same principles, naturally, would apply to selecting print media or radio.)

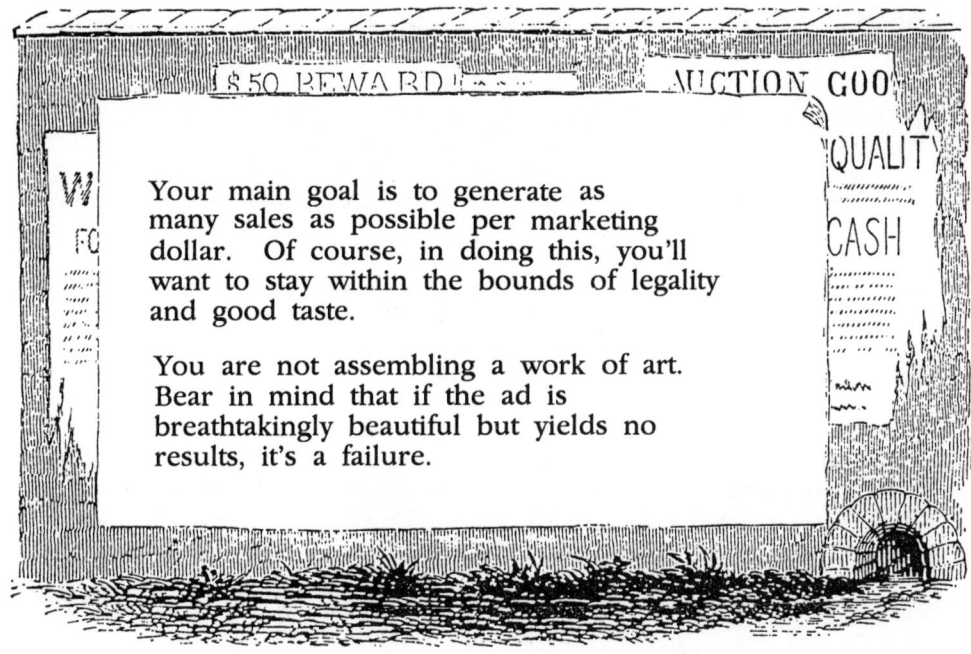

> Your main goal is to generate as many sales as possible per marketing dollar. Of course, in doing this, you'll want to stay within the bounds of legality and good taste.
>
> You are not assembling a work of art. Bear in mind that if the ad is breathtakingly beautiful but yields no results, it's a failure.

If it's a little brash and simplistic, but results in a 30% jump in your customer base, it's a success. You want maximum impact and tangible results. There are plenty of "dumb" commercials on television that run over and over again--at great expense--because they work.

Here are some rules followed by the "big guys" that will help you determine the main thrust of your ad. For our purposes, we'll assume you're planning a print display advertisement. Extensive broadcast publicity is often beyond the price range of most small businesses. The basic guidelines will probably help you to sharpen your overall message, whatever medium you select.

Assemble a "green sheet" of specifications about your ad. It should outline the product or service itself, the packaging, the pricing, and the medium you've selected. It should also feature the ad size, the duration of the ad, its costs, and as much information about your prospective customers as you can gather.

Follow the familiar AIDA formula: gain ATTENTION, develop INTEREST, generate DESIRE, initiate ACTION.

Develop a lead sentence. This sentence can shock the audience or make it laugh, ask a question or throw down a challenge. Whatever it does, however, your lead must stop people dead in their tracks. It cannot be longwinded. (This is often the most crucial component of any ad. You're strongly advised to come up with ten or fifteen candidates, and then select the strongest--preferably with trusted colleagues.)

Prove the claims of that lead sentence in the main text, or highlight key additional benefits of your product or service.

Speak the language of your customers throughout the ad.

Examine other successful ads and consider adapting their formats. You'll find that, in terms of page layout, the following rough rules of thumb have been proven quite successful:

> 1) Visuals, when used, should occupy at least 25% of your space, and perhaps as much as 50%.
>
> 2) Visuals usually work best beginning from the upper left-hand portion of the ad.
>
> 3) One of the most consistently successful advertising visuals: happy people using the product. Don't get too abstract unless you're feeling lucky.
>
> 4) Copy or selling points should come below the headline.

5) Text layout should feature between 25%-30% white space. Ads that are crammed with text alienate readers! Making the message accessible is usually a cost-effective choice.

(Note: The point above is ignored routinely by smaller businesses, with disastrous consequences. It's tempting to fill every square inch of that expensive space. Doing so, however, is extremely dangerous. "Jammed" messages represent a high percentage of the ads that don't work, can't deliver results, and never justify their cost.)

6) Keep it simple.

7) Closing copy should conclude with "action requests." Examples: "Get one next time you stop by the supermarket." "Try it today!" "Call 1-800-555-5555 for more information."

Now that you've got a rough idea how you want to proceed, it's time to judge your ad against the Million Dollar Checklist.

"How do the big corporations decide if an ad's worth spending money on?"

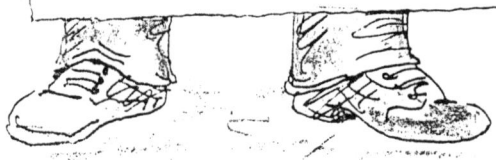

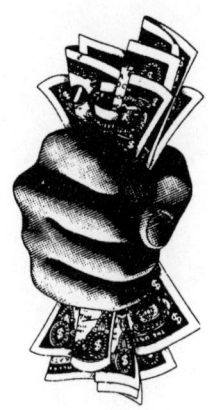

One of the answers is at your disposal right now: the Million Dollar Checklist.

The following pages contain 87 statements which may or may not apply to the ad you're planning to run.

When it comes to deciding whether to invest advertising dollars on a given ad, you should consider the following list pure gold. It can save you many expensive mistakes--mistakes you may well have the pleasure of watching your competitors make! The statements set out below are based on over ten million dollars worth of consumer research at many firms, and years of work from some of the best marketing minds in this country.

It's safe to say that no major nationwide ad campaign you'll ever see, or have seen in the last fifteen or twenty years, reached a "go" stage without someone, somewhere, consulting some aspect of the Million Dollar Checklist.

No ad of yours should reach a "go" stage until you consult the Checklist, either.

Go down the list, point-by-point, and give yourself one point for every "true" answer. No ad gets all "true" responses, but some do a lot better than others. Such ads represent a statistically smaller risk to the advertiser than the ideas that score poorly.

THE MILLION DOLLAR CHECKLIST

Supply each statement with a "true or false" response. Give your ad one point for each "true" answer.

The person who wrote the copy thoroughly knows the interests of the potential customers. (True/False)

The person who wrote the copy knows the product or service intimately. (True/False)

The copy appeals to major human motivators. (True/False)

The ad aims at specific types of people, and/or incorporates targeted marketing objectives. (True/False)

The ad spotlights the pleasure or self-preservation of persons who use the product or service. (True/False)

The ad promises satisfaction of a want or need, or a solution to a problem. (True/False)

The ad contrasts the benefit of the product or service with alternate promises. (True/False)

The opening paragraph of the copy contains news important to most prospects. (True/False)

The headline outlines a major customer benefit. (True/False)

The headline identifies and selects the customer. (True/False)

The headline states your brand name. (True/False)

The headline makes chief promises cheerfully. (True/False)

The headline conveys a short, clear idea. (True/False)

The headline contains fewer than twelve words. (True/False)

If the headline contains twelve or more words, it incorporates testimonials or quotes. (True/False)

The copy speaks comprehensibly to the prospect. (True/False)

The copy has an air of authenticity or genuineness, and does not sound artificial or "hyped." (True/False)

The copy describes the product or service. (True/False)

The copy describes how the product or service is used. (True/False)

The copy converts features of the product to customer benefits. (True/False)

The copy promises results--not things. (True/False)

The copy makes no ridiculous claims. (True/False)

The copy avoids overstatement. (True/False)

The copy provides proof of its claims. (True/False)

The copy emphasizes results rather than causes. (True/False)

The copy gives cause only to build belief. (True/False)

The copy is specific and avoids generalities. (True/False)

The copy follows the AIDA formula: gain ATTENTION, develop INTEREST, generate DESIRE, initiate ACTION. (True/False)

The copy gives the prospect an excuse to buy. (True/False)

The copy's opening sentence is clear and easy to follow. (True/False)

The copy's first idea is a short, compelling "grabber." (True/False)

The copy provides evidence to support its first idea. (True/False)

The copy tells a story. (True/False)

The copy tells a story using pictures featured in the ad. (True/False)

The copy provides facts promptly. (True/False)

The copy is long enough to cover the story it tells. (True/False)

The copy highlights and contrasts problems and solutions. (True/False)

The copy itemizes user benefits. (True/False)

The copy incorporates "bullets" and/or graphically interesting lists. (True/False)

The copy breaks text into sub-heads. (True/False)

The copy features a compelling guarantee. (True/False)

The copy features a slogan that describes or urges use of the product or service. (True/False)

The copy is laid out in small blocks of text. (True/False)

Most of the sentences use ten words or less. (True/False)

All unnecessary words have been deleted from the copy. (True/False)

The words used are not trite or bombastic. (True/False)

The copy--and the ad as a whole--uses many verbs and few adjectives. (True/False)

The copy--and the ad as a whole--uses only relevant words. (True/False)

The copy--and the ad as a whole--avoids abstraction and uncommon terms. (True/False)

The words used build a vision. (True/False)

The ad, taken as a whole, fits the medium selected. (True/False)

The ad is truth told with vigor and imagination. (True/False)

The ad is more earnest than glib. (True/False)

The ad appeals to both heart and mind. (True/False)

The ad is original and/or provocative. (True/False)

The ad relates easily to key prospects. (True/False)

The ad is simple, but not condescending. (True/False)

The ad is accurate, but not boastful. (True/False)

The overall feel of the ad is colloquial, natural, and friendly. (True/False)

The ad is frankly sales-oriented. (True/False)

The ad does not sound pretentious or aspire to be a piece of literature. (True/False)

The ad uses emotion that seems logical. (True/False)

The ad permits the prospect to make an emotional decision to buy that can be justified rationally. (True/False)

The ad is in good taste. (True/False)

The ad is disarmingly honest and forthright. (True/False)

The ad conveys a conversational, "person-to-person" feel. (True/False)

The ad, taken as a whole, is clear and understandable. (True/False)

The ad tends to use short, plain words. (True/False)

The ad avoids complex or confusing ideas. (True/False)

The ad is colorful and believable. (True/False)

The ad reaches a clear conclusion, at which point it attempts to turn interest to action. (True/False)

A decision to buy seems a natural conclusion of reading the ad. (True/False)

The ad tells prospects what to do. (True/False)

The ad openly suggests a purchase. (True/False)

The visuals used in the ad take up about as much space as the copy. (True/False)

The visuals used in the ad feature the product (or service) prominently. (True/False)

The visuals used in the ad highlight a clear benefit for the customer. (True/False)

The visuals used in the ad prove claims in the headline. (True/False)

The visuals used in the ad identify the product (or service) with a user. (True/False)

The visuals used in the ad feature happy people using the product (or service). (True/False)

The visuals used in the ad are dynamic and suggest action. (True/False)

The visuals used in the ad serve as an accessible "starting point" for the ad as a whole. (True/False)

The visuals used in the ad feature captions. (True/False)

If there are a number of visuals used in the ad, one is clearly dominant and more important than the others. (True/False)

The ad features one or more high-quality photographs, rather than drawings. (True/False)

The layout is clean and uncluttered. (True/False)

Approximately 25% of the entire ad is white space. (True/False)

Those working on the development of the ad are proud enough of the result to sign it. (True/False)

"I'm uncomfortable developing ad copy. Should I consider using an ad agency?"

Many people who are uncomfortable developing their own ad copy ask themselves this question. Here are the best guidelines for most small businesses.

Yes, if the agency is experienced, yet willing to charge a smaller client (such as your business) reduced rates on the strength of visible potential for later success.

No, if the options available to you are: a) a major agency at standard rates; b) your college roommate's brother-in-law who's just getting started; c) the guy down the street because he's convenient; or d) any old firm you locate through the yellow pages.

If you feel it's not appropriate for you to develop campaigns yourself, then the right agency can do you a world of good. Such a firm can help you find strong selling ideas, copy, and art, and can offer invaluable help in media selection.

How do I pick the agency? Here's a suggested checklist that will help you identify the firm that can give you the most bang for your buck. The advantage of the checklist approach is that it lists key items, lowering the odds that you'll forget something important. In addition, it judges all candidates by the same yardstick, helping you avoid overemotional decisions. Remember, though, that while you want to maintain a measure of objectivity, you should always give some heed to strong "gut feelings" about an organization.

Of course, you may have special agency needs for your product or service. You can always add or subtract items as your situation demands.

Sample checklist (Rating factors from zero to ten.)

FACTOR	Agency "A"	Agency "B"
Location (Easy service access?)	5	9
Size (Too big? Too small?)	8	4
Growth (Up? Down? Is the agency "steady"--or stagnant?)	7	6
Copy Experience (In your market?)	8	5
Art service (Enough diversity?)	8	4
Media services (Enough expertise in your market?)	7	3
Print vs. Broadcast experience/billing (Is the ratio right for you?)	3	4
Proficiency with "collaterals" such as brochures (Is the agency a "one-trick pony"?)	7	4
Sample ads (How do you rate their quality?)	9	7
Comments of other agencies (How do peers rate the firm?)	8	5

Comments of current clients (What's the "word on the street"?)	8	5
Affordability (Is the agency in your price range?)	8	5
Subjective factors (What's your "gut feeling" about the place?)	9	6
TOTAL	95	67

As we've noted, you may want to customize your series of checklist items. Here are some additional guideposts you might consider including: client turnover; number of clients your size; awards and special accomplishments; and general agency orientation.

When auditioning agencies, you're likely to encounter a certain amount of wining and dining. Be impressed, but only a little. Remember, these are people who make their living selling things to other people. Don't get swept off your feet by the first wave of dog and pony shows. What really counts is what they can (and are willing) to do to help you grow.

If you don't have a lot of dollars to throw around, probably radio. Again, however, it is worth pointing out that, for many businesses, no advertising at all is the best option. If you are determined to follow a strict, well thought out plan, however, to meet legitimate goals that can only be obtained through paid broadcast media, then you should take a close look at radio. (Bear in mind, however, that print advertising can also be extremely cost-effective.)

While television carries undeniable impact, it does not offer you something that radio does. With radio, you have the opportunity to come off as big as IBM . . . affordably!

On television, production values will play a huge role in determining the success of your spot. High quality is somewhat easier to attain on radio, and much less expensive. Another factor arguing in radio's favor: it invades, interrupts, stops listeners, often in a dramatic way. And the "seams" between radio's main programming and its commercial messages are usually less noticeable than television's.

Radio often pinpoints specific markets more efficiently than television can, though its reach is not as impressive in terms of raw numbers.

Finally, radio stations in your area may well have more competition than the television stations do. Stations with many rivals are more likely to offer competitive terms for the spots you air. Shop around. Then compare the cost per thousand listeners, not just the fee the station would charge you.

1) Compose at least ten scripts for every ad you plan to air. Pick the best one.

2) The first five seconds of the ad, more than any other segment, will determine its success or failure. Make sure you have a powerful "kicker."

3) One minute of air time should allow you to get through 125 words; thirty seconds, something over 60. That's not many words. Make them count. Highlight consumer benefits.

4) Use sound effects (SFX) to gain attention and get your message across.

5) The announcer(s) you use should project enthusiasm; keep the tone conversational, perhaps even breezy. In short, make the message easy to listen to.

6) Listen for successful scripts and techniques in ads that have already proven their success on the radio; try to emulate them.

7) Repeat the message for greatest impact.

8) Measure your results!

PERSONAL SELLING FOR SUCCESS
(OR: POOR SALESPEOPLE HAVE SKINNY KIDS!)

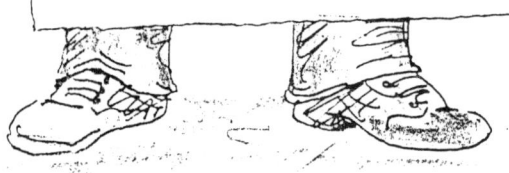

"I'm going to be doing a lot of our company's in-person selling work. Any suggestions?"

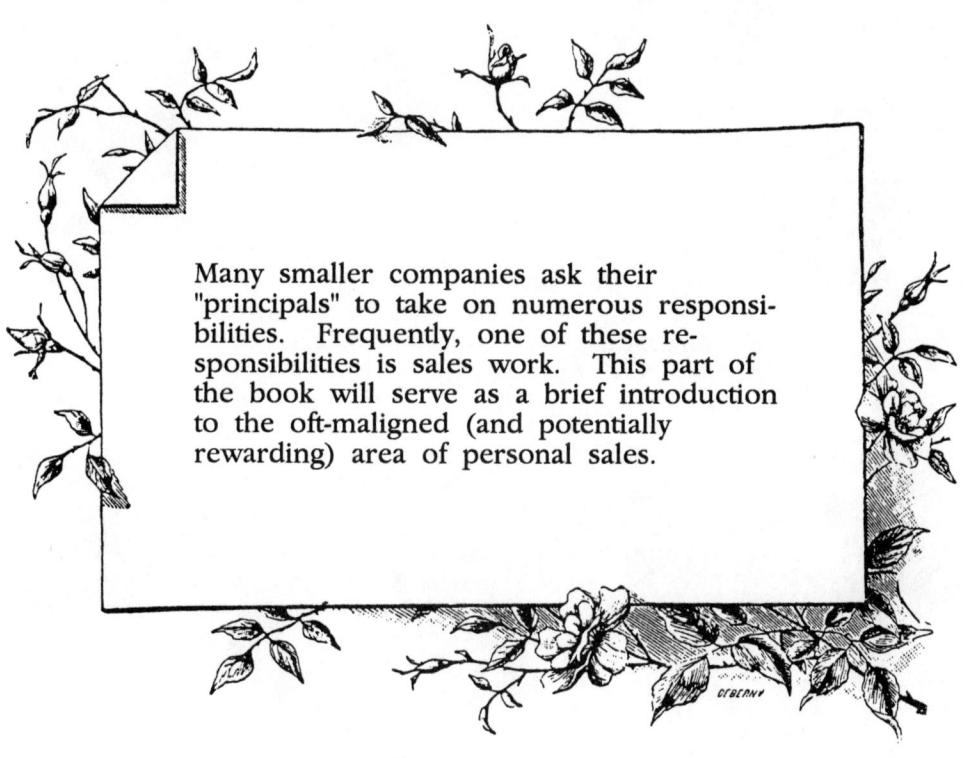

Many smaller companies ask their "principals" to take on numerous responsibilities. Frequently, one of these responsibilities is sales work. This part of the book will serve as a brief introduction to the oft-maligned (and potentially rewarding) area of personal sales.

Once upon a time, a young man visiting New York City for the first time stopped a sweet-looking little old lady on the street to ask directions. "Excuse me, ma'am," he said politely, "but would you know how I'd get to Carnegie Hall?" The woman looked at him, smiled, and said, "Practice, my boy . . . practice."

Those words are good advice for beginning salespeople, as well. Practice. Practice. Practice. And it's probably a good idea to add one more injunction: Prepare.

Perhaps the best course a beginning salesperson can take is to do a great deal of roleplaying. Find a colleague to work with, then develop your technique with him or her. Make sure you're not just confronting the easy objections and client types; strive for realism. The advantage to this approach is the opportunity to make your mistakes (and there will be mistakes) in a risk-free environment. You'll learn while your revenue isn't on the line. Practice selling until you're sick of it; that's when you'll start to become effective.

It certainly does. Here's how.

(You'll find a condensed review of the principles of management by objective on page 46.)

 Your situation is a potential customer's existing opinions and buying habits.

 Your objective is to make a sale.

 Your potential strategies come down to a number of professionally-oriented steps you can take. They're listed on the next page.

1) Do your homework. Know your product backwards and forwards. Know what your prospects want.

2) Never forget to think like a customer. The best way to achieve your goal (a sale) is to keep your eye on the prospect's goals--and help him or her meet them.

3) Establish a personal bond. Where appropriate, use first names. People hate doing business with strangers. Strive for genuine interpersonal contact.

4) Take notes and draw diagrams for your prospect. This keeps the conversation moving and puts you in a position of control.

5) Don't rely heavily on jargon or technology. It alienates people and loses sales. Aim for clear, simple communication. Leave no doubts whatsoever about how you can solve the prospect's problems. Emphasize results.

6) If you use flip charts, keep them simple. They should incorporate no more than ten words per page, and utilize illustrations with color.

7) Don't be arrogant or disrespectful; stay friendly and informal. Successful salespeople never come off as academic or superior.

8) Listen. And never argue. The prospective customer's perceptions are the only ones that matter.

9) Emphasize tangible product benefits. The more immediate and relevant to "real-world" experience, the better.

10) Work with your prospect. He or she may well have to "sell" the boss on the idea. Though it's preferable to try to present directly to decision-makers, it's not always possible. Back off when appropriate. Provide all necessary information.

11) After the groundwork has been laid, and interest in your product or service has been established, ask for the order. What's the worst that could happen? They might say "no." That's not the end of the world.

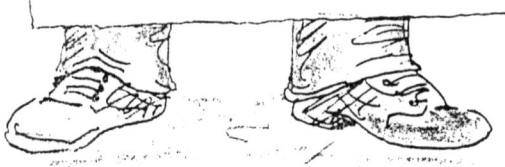

That depends on what you're selling, to whom, and under what conditions. However, some general guidelines will apply.

Outline the pitch thoroughly. Set everything up on paper. Then tear it apart and start over again. Find the version that's right for you.

Emphasize compelling facts through the use of endorsements. "Our service increased the profitability of Company X." (Be sure to clear this with the people at Company X--perhaps informally.)

Highlight problems and solutions. These are the terms in which most good managers think. Put your ideas in their language.

Speak loudly, clearly, and plainly. You can't sell to a person who can't understand you. Good diction and strong speaking skills project confidence--a key selling trait.

Stay away from "I" and "me"--emphasize "you." The terms you use do a lot to convey messages about whose side you're really on. Stack the odds in your favor; give the prospect every opportunity to understand that you're seeing things from his or her vantage point.

The pitch does not stand alone, but must be preceded with a discussion of the prospect's needs, past experience, and expectations. Once that's been done, the moment of truth could sound something like this:

"Mr. Brown, you mentioned in your dinner speech last week that one of your major problems was the fact that too many untested, unproven items make it onto your store shelves, with disappointing results. Am I right?"

(What's he going to say? "No"? Of course not. "Yes" responses from your prospect, even in response to questions not directly related to the sale, strengthen your presentation. However: be sure not to misquote the prospect at any point.)

"Well, Mr. Brown, Classic Touch Bread just may be your solution--and the answer to the problem of increasing sales and profits."

(A solution! Not only that, a solution offered promptly and professionally, in terms of Mr. Brown's goals--not ours.)

"You very reasonably asked for proof . . . and Classic Touch can offer just that. Here's a chart showing what we've done with this brand in three other markets. These are the names and addresses of the dealers who stock it now. I'm sure they'd be very happy to talk with you about how their profits increased on a square-foot basis."

(Successful businesspeople tend to be skeptical. That's no problem. Point out where your product, program, or service has worked before. Supply names and addresses where appropriate.)

"And right here, Mr. Brown, are some in-store photos of our displays. This particular display has a $20 value, and it's free to you with your first order."

(A good incentive can turn an interested prospect into a customer. Often, such an offer can supply the rational basis for going ahead and purchasing from you--consolidating the emotional bond you've established.)

"I know you're a busy man, Mr. Brown, and I want you to know I very much appreciate your taking the time to talk to me today. Would you like one display each for all ten of your stores?"

(This is where beginning salespeople get nervous. Never mind--just ask for the sale. It's by far the most effective method once you've established that your prospect has a valid interest in your product or service.)

Be prepared to go into more detail--just in case Mr. Brown says something other than "Yes, please." He may ask for more particulars on your test, or details on prices, or scheduling, all of which are excellent signs. As a general rule, the more you can get prospects to talk about their needs, their businesses, or their potential use of your product or service, the better.

Note:

Many prospects, particularly managers and professional people, will say something like, "Well, we'll think about it." This is not necessarily a bad sign. After all, your prospect has probably been entrusted with huge resources . . . and such people tend to shy away from snap decisions. It's no crime to have your proposal viewed as a business proposal, one not immediately accepted or rejected. Your door stands ajar. Follow up with a pleasant phone call or letter . . . and then try again later.

Telemarketing has proved effective in recent years for a wide range of companies. But actual results depend on the soundness of the methods used. Your efforts will depend, in large part, on the overall plan, the delivery style, and the content.

Of the three, style may have the greatest influence on a telemarketing campaign's success or failure. As in most other forms of communication, a persuasive "package" may tilt the odds in your favor.

Two key problems facing telemarketers are: 1) most people you reach are doing other things, and consider your call an interruption; and 2) you must often deal with the frustration the prospect remembers from the unsuccessful (and often amateurish) telemarketing efforts of other organizations--exchanges your contact is probably not eager to repeat.

"Cold" telemarketing is, by its very nature, likely to annoy many of the people it reaches. The successful telemarketer, however, develops a winning mind-set that neutralizes this problem.

Your approach must be one that takes the odds into account. Think: "I can put together an excellent presentation, and a large number of the people I talk to will still turn me down flat--some more politely than others. Still, every 'no' answer just gets that rejection out of the way, and eventually allows me to move on to a 'yes.'"

Be ready for the "no" answer, and don't let it bother you. Just look forward to what the next call has to offer. If necessary, take frequent breaks. Don't take each call so seriously that it impairs your effectiveness. Thin-skinned people tend not to make good telemarketers.

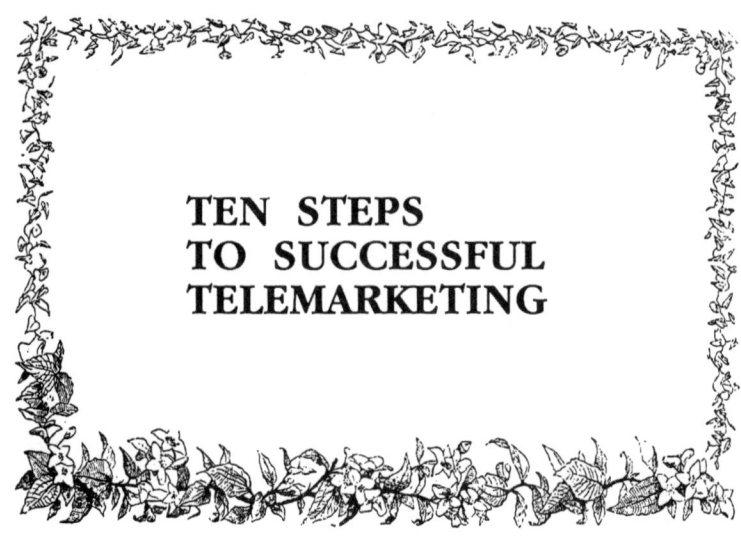

TEN STEPS TO SUCCESSFUL TELEMARKETING

1) Develop a script you feel comfortable with and stick to it.

2) Be sure you are using a pleasant, relaxed tone of voice. This, more than any other factor, will help you make a success out of the first crucial seconds--where most calls are won or lost.

3) Identify yourself clearly and briefly, then continue with your pitch.

4) Get the person involved in a discussion, preferably with "yes-answer questions": "Is this Charles Brown?" "Mr. Brown, do you own a car?" "Is your address 123 Elm Street?"

5) Having gained even the most apparently insignificant response, realize that you've gained a victory. Expand on the success. Respond positively, with mild enthusiasm: "Oh, good." "Great." "That's good to hear." Then continue.

6) Use problem and solution statements: "Naturally, you don't want your home value to drop . . . and Jones Decorating Service can be an easy, low-cost solution."

7) Don't wait or pause. Fill the holes.

8) Have a script--but work it so thoroughly that you don't sound like you're reading.

9) Paint a mental picture wherever you can--make the caller's imagination work for you.

10) Ask for the order (or to schedule an in-person visit).

In two words, satisfy customers. Specifically, you should:

Always come through as promised on the initial order. Flawless first presentations are often sabotaged by late delivery, poor quality, rude phone exchanges, etcetera. Don't let it happen. The first-time customer is at a crucial stage; if you ignore his priorities, you'll find yourself out one return customer.

Recognize that your customers (particularly managers and other professionals) have personal goals, such as power, prestige, and position security. Bear these in mind as you develop the relationship.

Follow up. Stop in to see how the product or service is working out. Make note of any problems. This not only helps in the use of the product or service, but also helps you build up professional credibility.

Speak the prospect's language throughout the relationship. Bankers, for instance, feel comfortable dealing with figures. They think in terms of sales . . . profits . . . costs . . . return on investment . . . realistic forecasts that match known cases. At any given point in your business relationship, therefore, you must remember that if you speak to these points, bankers, as a rule, will usually tune in to you very well. Talk dreams, generalities, and broad concepts, and you lose them. The principle applies to many different groups of customers; don't make the mistake of assuming you needn't see things from the other person's perspective once you've closed a sale.

> The president of one of the world's most successful hotel chains was asked about the key to her success. She answered: "Well, one of the major steps I took was to stop asking people to be nice. Instead, I hired nice people."

The right salespeople can make all the difference. Good performers offer the possibility of tremendous paybacks. They also greatly reduce all sorts of customer relations problems that occur with poor salespeople. The good ones are well worth the extra effort it takes to find them.

When you decide you want to hire a new salesperson, go all out. Any personnel decision is important, but salespeople, because they can add so much to your bottom line virtually immediately, deserve special attention. Interview at least five or ten applicants for every one position.

Check references and associates thoroughly. Make sure you've got a good potential "fit."

As you go over each candidate's background and qualifications, strive to give and obtain valid, useful information about your goals and those of the salesperson. If you can't hire the person, try at least to make friends. After all, odds are such applicants will get a job somewhere. Never burn bridges; your "friend" may turn out to be a valued contact somewhere down the line.

During the interview process, make every effort to stay objective and honest. Draw up a list of the ten most important qualities you'd like to see the new person display: articulate, ethical, persuasive, etcetera. Then rate each applicant against the list. At the end of all the interviews, add up each candidate's "check marks." If one person easily outclasses the rest of the field, your decision will be pretty easy.

(This "check mark" system is used by some of the largest corporations in the country to find sales "tigers.")

Finally, remember what Mark Twain said about marriage. It applies, in large measure, to hiring, too. Twain wrote that a marriage "should be entered into with one's eyes wide open beforehand . . . and half closed afterwards."

Any salesperson's compensation package should convey the message, "You are wanted and appreciated." It's important to keep in mind, though, that few people work for money alone.

Issues of job satisfaction, personal fulfillment, and self-image enter into the equation. Some incentive factors have highly variable, intangible, or indirect costs to your company. These would include: company social activities; training and development; fringe benefits; closer proximity to key decision-makers; and so on.

Nevertheless, with most salespeople, money should act as a powerful incentive. The aim is to create as much motivation as possible.

What are the options? There are a number of possibilities, each with its own advantages and disadvantages.

1) Straight salary. It's straightforward, simple, and easy to keep track of, but it offers little or no incentive to excel.

2) Straight commission. Incentive is high, but it limits your control over such issues as attendance. This method of compensation can distance you from your sales staff. If someone's failing, virtually nothing will convince that person to stay on with you. If someone's doing well, they'll be tempted to think of themselves as an independent operator.

3) Draw against projected sales. This guarantees a predictable monthly income to the salesperson, and allows increased pay for top performance. It can be expensive, though; you pay full "salary" even to those who eventually don't work out.

4) Salary plus commission. This approach certainly motivates people, and can be customized for each salesperson to provide maximum control. Careful planning is still necessary, however.

5) Salary plus profit-sharing program. It can help build "team spirit," but may have a negative impact from the salesperson's perspective. Sales is often fiercely competitive and individualistic, and many sales reps will resent the fact that such plans are influenced by the actions of many others.

6) Salary plus stock options. If your company provides the right setting, this can be highly effective. This technique should be viewed primarily as a long-term incentive.

7) Salary plus points toward "high-ticket" prizes. The advantage here is that motivation for top performance can come not only from the office environment, but also from the salesperson's home. The technique tends to work best, however, only with certain types of personalities; many are turned off by the idea, and can even consider it somewhat demeaning.

A close check of the plans in place at your two or three strongest competitors will give you some guidance in selecting the best plan. Such research will probably expose you to plans that are functioning well and have been thoroughly tested. Consider adopting similar or identical approaches.

"How do I keep salespeople motivated?"

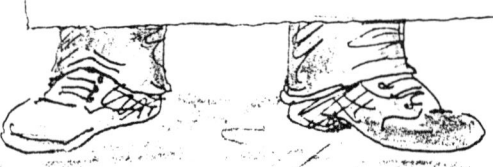

Most good managers try to hire people who are both willing and able. Training can build ability, but willingness is sometimes more difficult to engender over the long haul. The fact is, virtually all salespeople--even the very best--need motivation from time to time.

Here are some of the best ways to keep people enthused.

1) Challenge them. In effect, say, "I believe in you; you can do it!"

2) Work with them in setting goals. The targets you come up with will be more meaningful.

3) Show respect. Everyone craves it, and very few of us get as much as we deserve.

4) Hold regular meetings with your sales staff. State main objectives; summarize them; outline long-term goals. Then LISTEN to the reaction. Let salespeople play a role in your planning.

5) Give people honest, appreciative recognition--privately and publicly. Awards, certificates, plaques, prizes . . . these things really do make a difference.

6) Where there are problems, provide upbeat, enthusiastic coaching. Cast yourself as the salesperson's ally: "You and I will solve this problem. We made a mistake with customer X, but we can correct that. What are your thoughts on this?"

7) Don't hang over people's desks, monitoring every phone call. Give them some freedom. They'll perform better.

Answer: very carefully!

What is your goal? To get rid of someone who isn't performing? Yes. But there are other important factors you have to take into account, as well. You want to minimize the ill-will and trauma both of you will feel. And you want to replace this person with an optimistic, productive, top-notch player. That's hard to do if a negative, crisis atmosphere hangs over you as you enter the hiring process.

In virtually all situations, then, you can't just walk up to the person and say, "You're fired." Remember, too, that others on your sales staff will closely monitor the comings and goings of their colleagues; morale can plunge (and rumors can magnify events out of all proportion) when firing is handled badly.

(It's probably worth noting here that, in every firing situation, there is a possibility that the discharged employee will bring a lawsuit against you or your firm for wrongful dismissal. Even frivolous court cases can cost you time and money, so you should probably discuss such situations with your attorney BEFORE making a decision to fire a salesperson.)

HERE ARE SOME GUIDELINES that have proven effective over the years.

Don't make a decision to fire someone until you've exhausted every possible avenue that might lead to improved performance. Firing is a last resort, and it's often most effective as an unplayed "trump card."

Don't accuse someone of a generality (such as "not fitting in" or "needing some more hustle") without offering clear ways to solve the problems you define. Discuss the specific complaint you have. Work out a plan to correct it. Set target dates. If the goals aren't met, or, worse, if the salesperson makes no effort to work with you, it may be time to cut the string.

When the time comes to end the relationship, minimize negative feelings and confrontational tactics. These are now obsolete. Try to reduce stress on both sides, and avoid making an enemy. (Making enemies is unproductive and bad for business.)

Briefly review all the efforts made on each side to make things work out. Avoid finger-pointing or assigning blame. Acknowledge, if appropriate, that a genuine effort was made. Also take the time to recognize any strong points (such as showing up for work regularly or good rapport with the rest of the office.)

Then point out that, despite everyone's best intentions, production levels haven't been satisfactory--despite repeated efforts to correct problems.

Finally, get to the point and announce your decision. Over the years, as you might imagine, thousands of companies have had to grapple with the problem of firing well-intentioned people. Thanks to the contributions of many managers, a tactful yet effective "script" has emerged, and it's a real help when it comes to delivering the final difficult words. Here's what it sounds like.

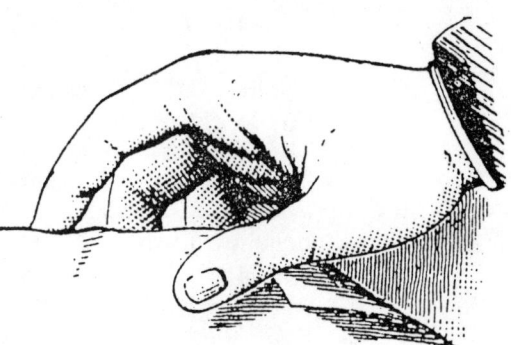

"Because of all this, Charlie, it looks like I must reluctantly say that we have to part company. You have many good qualities and I'm sure you'll be able to do well at any number of other jobs. But this position just isn't your cup of tea. I guess what I'm saying is, right now, you're sort of like a square peg in a round hole. Now, that's not the fault of the peg or the hole; but, by the same token, it's not good for either side to continue trying to make something like that work out, either."

Remember to ...

Listen to the comments the salesperson has, but keep your composure as you do so. They may be bitter words, but they may also contain information you should be aware of. Remember--half of the problem here is almost certainly on your side. It is management's responsibility to see that the selection methods used in hiring employees in the first place are sound. Moreover, it's your job to keep employees challenged, well trained, and clear on goals and procedures. If the relationship hasn't worked out, so be it: but learn what you can from the mistakes on each side.

Let the person work off some steam. Your response to that should be praise, not more pointless attack. "Hey, you did the best you could. I realize that." "This job just wasn't right for you. You may well end up with a much better deal." "I think you have a lot to offer, and because of that I really want us to part as friends."

Offer, wherever appropriate, to write a measured and useful letter of recommendation. You might even be in a position to help the person find that next job.

If you can, allow plenty of time for the transition. Two weeks is recommended.

Don't fire instinctively! This is definitely one of those decisions you can't rush. Ending a business relationship is a traumatic undertaking, and you probably won't want to do it any more than you have to.

PINCHING EVERY PENNY: HOW TO SAVE MONEY IN PLACES YOU NEVER THOUGHT YOUR BUSINESS COULD

It isn't easy, but many businesses manage to do this. How? Bartering and "payment in kind."

The key is to offer reciprocal benefits to the person with whom you're dealing. If you publish a quarterly newsletter with good circulation among calendar manufacturers, you may be able to offer your printer (assuming he or she produces calendars) a sizeable advertisement in lieu of payment (or receive a substantial discount). Similarly, if you offer interior design services, and need help setting up a desktop publishing system, you may be in a position to set up a similar arrangement with a consultant specializing in hardware and software selection--if the consultant is in need of an office makeover.

If you have a product that is uniquely useful in a number of business applications, there's a greater likelihood that you'll be able to establish a "payment in kind" arrangement. A software design firm may be able to interest suppliers in a dollar-for-dollar exchange of goods if one of the firm's new packages represents a real breakthrough available nowhere else.

Bartering isn't something you can expect to establish with a large percentage of your vendors. There's nothing you can do if the match is bad between what you do and what your contact needs. Unfortunately, this is likely to be the case quite often.

Nevertheless, many alert proprietors have set up what some might consider out-of-the ordinary arrangements that saved large sums of money. Keep your eyes open, and don't be afraid to ask; the worst that can happen is that someone can say no.

Usually, if you're a retailer, all you have to do is ask. Manufacturers and wholesalers, as a rule, have a wide variety of consumer display and in-store advertising materials they'd love to get into your hands. If for some reason a major supplier hasn't offered the flyers, literature, prepacks, or aisle displays you'd like to use, a letter to its home office will usually do the trick.

Judging the effectiveness of these materials is another matter. Not everything will increase sales, and if your floor or booth space is limited, you'll want to maximize your results and do as little experimenting as you can. After all, those are real, live customers strolling through your store--not focus group members.

Fortunately, you can let others do the research work for you; here's how. Contact a retailer in your field who's not a competitor of yours. (Most people get in touch with businesses in another city.) Ask if he or she has tried display "A," and, if so, what kind of results it delivered. Repeat the process as often as you want with new contacts. You may even learn of high-profit displays that you hadn't considered!

Let the other guy make the mistakes, and then make your best display and in-store advertising decisions.

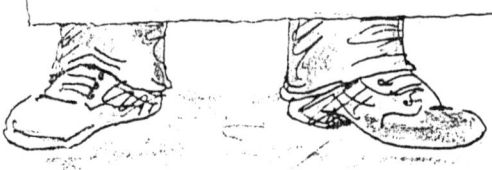

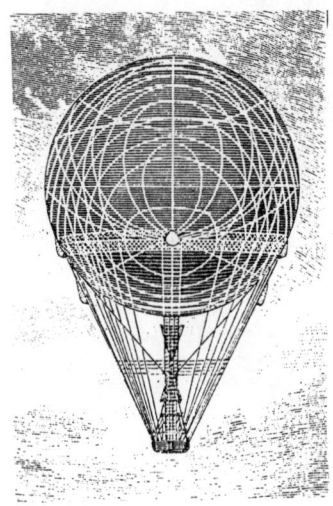

You can, and many businesses (especially retailers) do.

The key is cooperative advertising, and for many companies it's available at little or no cost. Here's how it works: If you sell widgets that you buy from the Top-Notch Widget Corporation, you may be able to get the manufacturer and/or distributor with which you work to run a newspaper ad that prominently features Top Notch's widgets--and your address! There's a chance that you'll be able to take advantage of a program that already exists. Find out from your suppliers.

The reason so many of the larger manufacturers and related organizations are willing to go with this approach is simple. They need you. Those businesses that deal directly with the consumer are of immense importance in the "chain" that begins at the factory and ends at your cash register. If they can target a viable retail outlet toward which they can steer qualified customers, sales go up--and everyone's happy.

Of course, every setting is different, and not every business is in a position to reap the benefits of cooperative advertising. But for many, finding out if there's a program that can help boost sales for nothing or next-to-nothing is an excellent idea.

Simple.

Watch their commercials.

Don't watch them as a consumer would, though. Watch them as an advertiser might; as an entrepreneur might. Look! There's Megafoods, Incorporated, taking out an ad on the nightly network news. They've made a decision to spend a great deal of money to broadcast one thirty-second message. They probably did not make that decision without careful analysis of market trends, consumer groups, and the competitive business environment in which they work. There probably won't be a perfect match between your business and theirs, but you may well be able to pick out important trends--at no cost--that can help you in your marketing work.

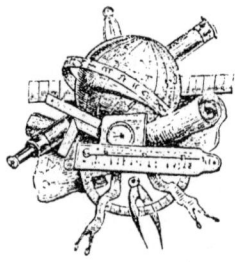

Use your VCR to record commercials you see run repeatedly. Then review them carefully. You'll be taking advantage of thousands of dollars worth of market research work.

Who does the ad speak to? (In virtually all cases, it is not "the general public," but rather a discrete segment of it.) What is the intended audience's age? Income level? Educational background? How does the message gain that group's attention? What interests or predispositions does the spot exploit? What concerns does the ad address?

Many people subscribe to the popular myth that advertising (and particularly advertising in the mass media) dictates tastes and preferences to its audience. Nothing could be more wrong. If advertisers could do that they would be hypnotists, not marketers, and the millions upon millions of dollars spent yearly on audience research and consumer preference studies would represent an expensive exercise in idiocy. Advertisers can motivate, inform, and persuade, but they can't compel. And they cannot do anything until they listen with rapt attention to the needs, interests, and predispositions of their intended audience.

You may have had the experience of watching an advertisement on television and thinking to yourself, "That must be the stupidest commercial I've ever seen in my life." You may even ask yourself why the advertiser continues to run such an obviously inferior ad over and over again. If the ad came from a major manufacturer or was designed by a prominent agency, it's a good bet that it was not produced before its underlying ideas were tested extensively with consumers. The "stupid ad" was almost certainly compared to dozens of other candidates, and found to deliver superior results. And the very fact that you see the ad again and again is testimony to the fact that it works! Why would anyone pay to repeat an ad that didn't?

One of the most important points to remember in this area is that Procter and Gamble, IBM, McDonald's, or any of the other major advertisers don't care about producing art. They care about reaching and motivating consumers who are likely to buy their products. By watching how larger organizations do just that, you can discover important market facts and consumer trends that will help your business reach out in the same effective way to its customers.

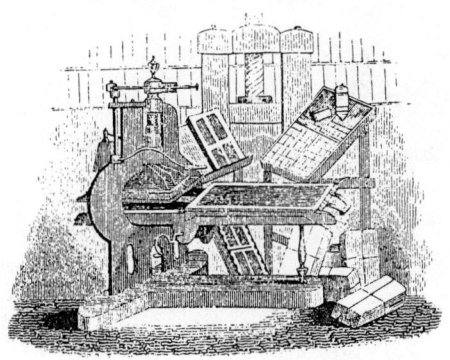

You don't have to spend a fortune to get superior results from your catalog, mailers, and related promotional materials.

One of the best moves you can make is to secure, either through purchase or rental, a good desktop publishing system. You're living in the information age--take advantage of it! By investing in a good-quality computer system and the appropriate software, and by taking the time to get up and running with it, you can save yourself thousands of dollars in future typesetting costs. For most applications, the laser-jet quality such systems provide is quite adequate, and the technology is improving every day.

Do not hire outside typesetters except as a last resort. The following chart will show why.

OBJECTIVE: Clean, professional-looking catalog.

CANDIDATES: Typesetter versus laser-jet publishing system.

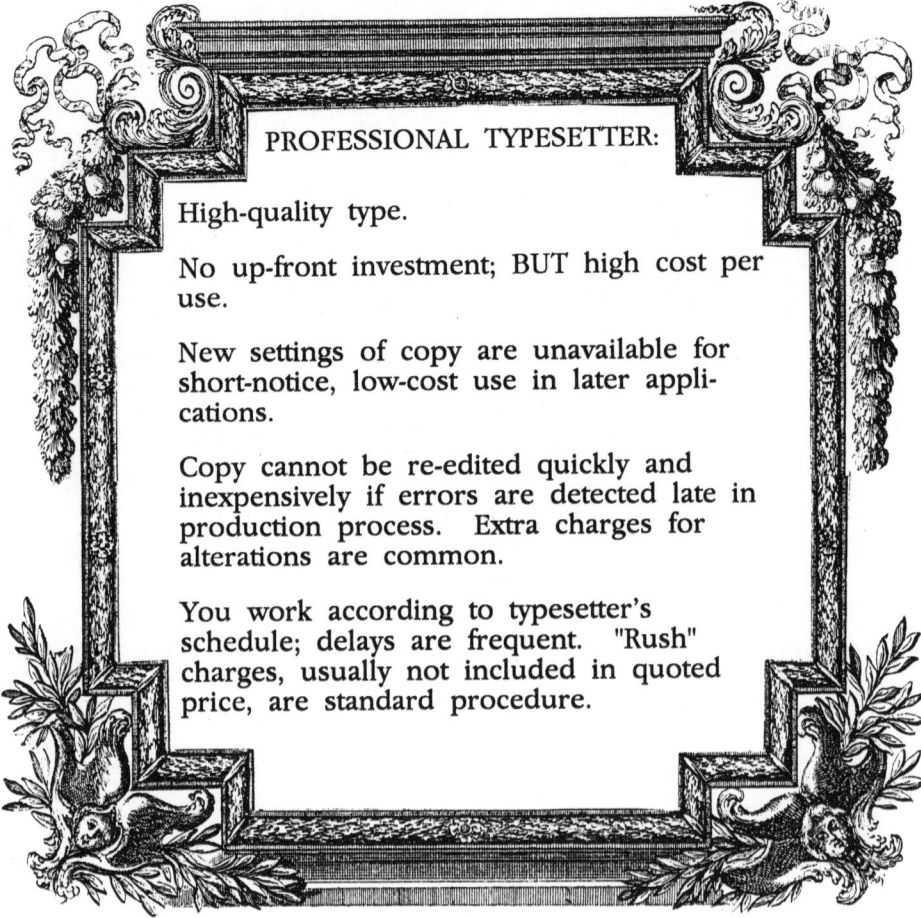

PROFESSIONAL TYPESETTER:

High-quality type.

No up-front investment; BUT high cost per use.

New settings of copy are unavailable for short-notice, low-cost use in later applications.

Copy cannot be re-edited quickly and inexpensively if errors are detected late in production process. Extra charges for alterations are common.

You work according to typesetter's schedule; delays are frequent. "Rush" charges, usually not included in quoted price, are standard procedure.

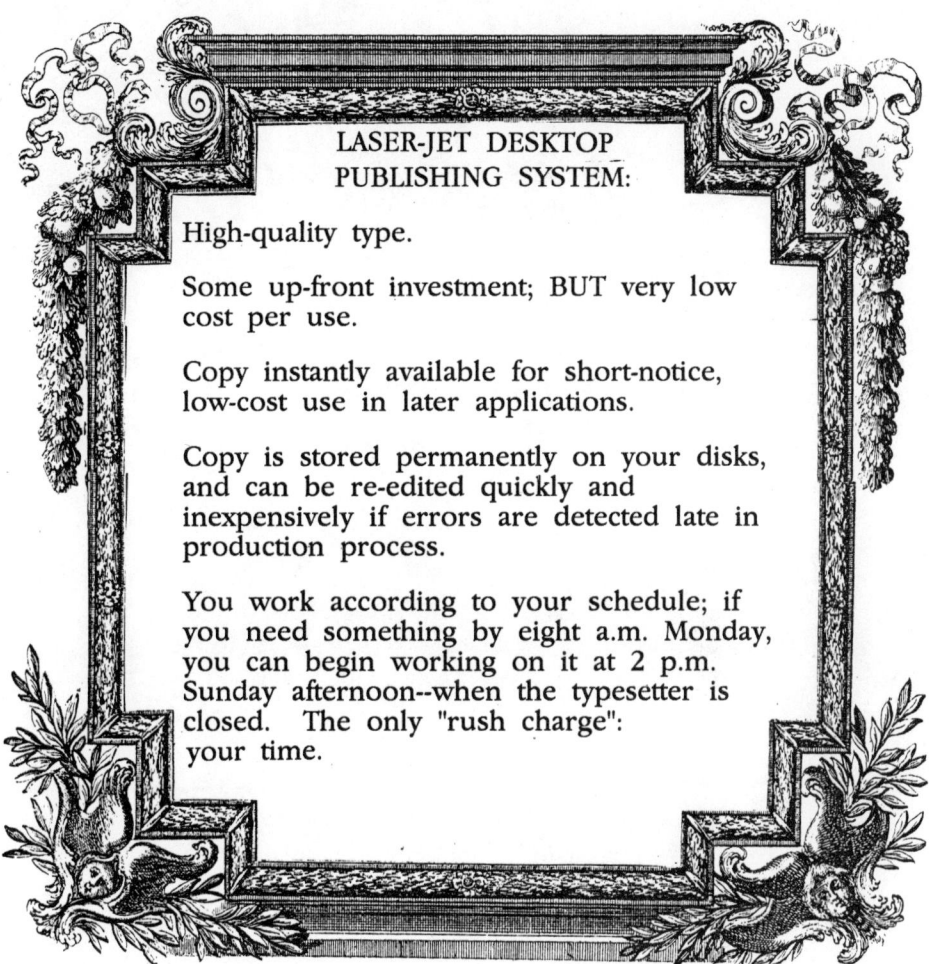

LASER-JET DESKTOP PUBLISHING SYSTEM:

High-quality type.

Some up-front investment; BUT very low cost per use.

Copy instantly available for short-notice, low-cost use in later applications.

Copy is stored permanently on your disks, and can be re-edited quickly and inexpensively if errors are detected late in production process.

You work according to your schedule; if you need something by eight a.m. Monday, you can begin working on it at 2 p.m. Sunday afternoon--when the typesetter is closed. The only "rush charge": your time.

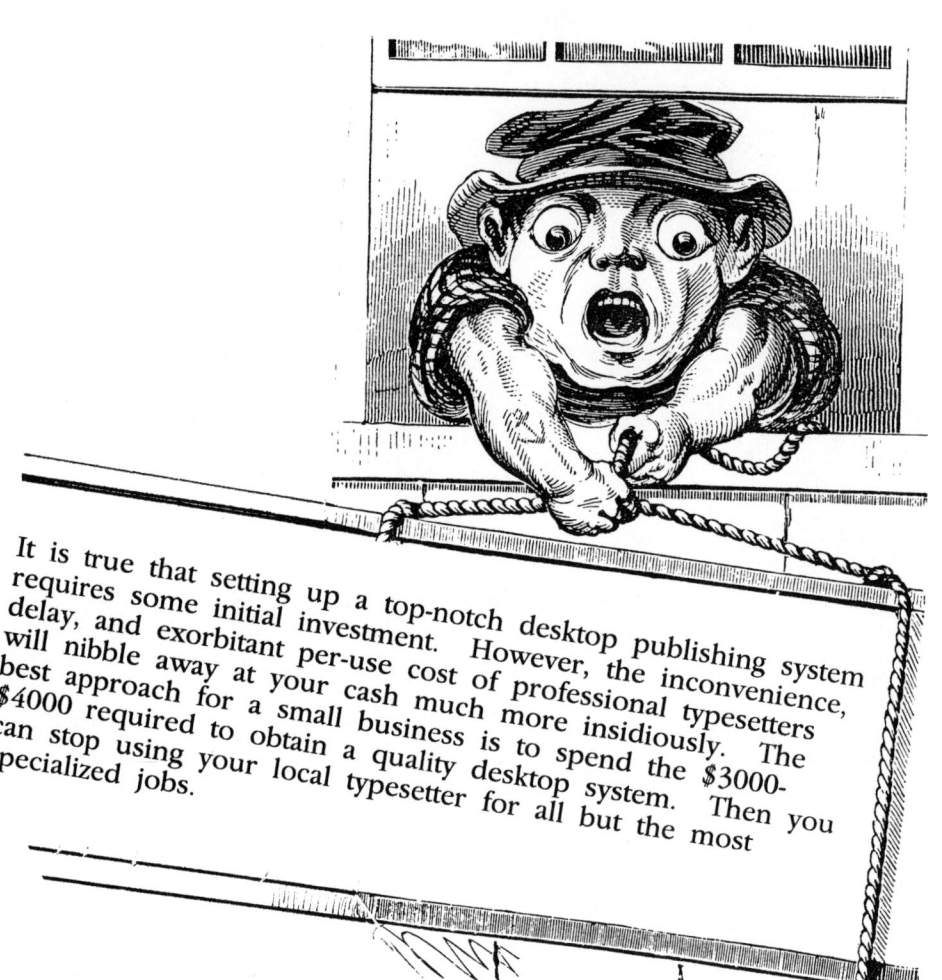

It is true that setting up a top-notch desktop publishing system requires some initial investment. However, the inconvenience, delay, and exorbitant per-use cost of professional typesetters will nibble away at your cash much more insidiously. The best approach for a small business is to spend the $3000-$4000 required to obtain a quality desktop system. Then you can stop using your local typesetter for all but the most specialized jobs.

Of course, if you already have a computer, there's a very good chance that all you'll need is a laser-jet printer and one of the better software packages. There are many from which to choose. Whatever you do, see what the system looks like in action. Don't just rely on brochures or sales pitches. You must determine how well or poorly a given package suits your needs before you buy it. Once you're up and running, you're going to be spending a good deal of time working with the system, and it will probably be too late to make major changes without expense.

"How can I get a hot mailing list without spending any money at the list broker houses?"

The lists you can buy (or, more accurately, rent) from the large mailing list houses have several disadvantages. They age quickly, so you can't hold on to them for any longer than, say, a month without the list losing some of its value. Furthermore, you can usually only use the lists once; they're "seeded" with false labels to weed out people who violate their contract with the list house by mailing multiple times. Finally, they're inconvenient. You have to make many phonecalls and deal with unfamiliar industry terms in deciding just which list you want to use.

Here is the ultimate irony: many businesses go through all of that without taking advantage of the very best mailing list they could possibly use. This list is available free of charge. It can be used as many times as is necessary without violating any contract provisions. And it points the company using it toward highly qualified prospects--even though its selection requires no knowledge of industry jargon or technical terms.

It is, of course, the list of your current customers. With the advent of affordable personal computer systems, there is now no excuse to let the vitally important information that is contained on your invoices lumber unused. Put the information to work. Obtain a good-quality database management software program (there are some excellent "shareware" versions available on a voluntary payment basis; see the chapter on software elsewhere in this book). Then make your customer list your first choice in mailings-- and for telemarketing work and in-person sales as well.

(Even if you don't have a personal computer, you can take advantage of internal customer lists. Simply type up the names onto a 8 1/2" x 11" sheet of labels. Then have them photocopied onto identical sheets at your local copy shop.)

You'll see results quickly from this "no-budget" approach. That's because the people you'll reach have already expressed enough interest in your products or services to purchase them! How much more "qualified" can a list get? A "live" list is one of your company's most important assets. Failing to use it effectively is equivalent to throwing money out your office window.

For many companies, there is a cost-effective alternative to leasing lists from the big mailing houses--even if your in-house list wouldn't reach your intended audience.

Like most businesses, your company probably subscribes to a trade publication of some sort. This is a periodical intended solely for a narrow (but, within the given field, crucial) audience. BILLBOARD is the trade publication for professionals in the music industry. ADVERTISING AGE addresses those in the advertising field.

Many of these publications are difficult if not impossible to obtain through standard magazine and newspaper outlets, and therein lies your opportunity. Most of the readers of these periodicals receive their copies through subscription only. If your target group can be identified by its readership of one

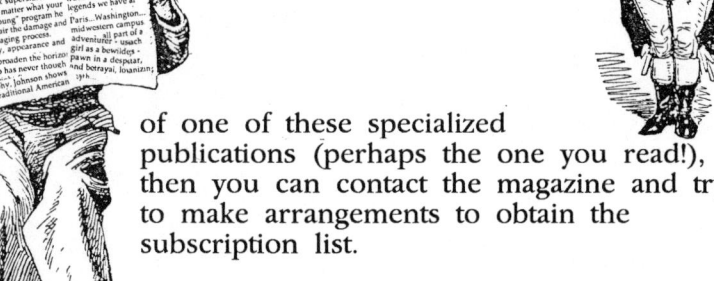

of one of these specialized publications (perhaps the one you read!), then you can contact the magazine and try to make arrangements to obtain the subscription list.

It's preferable to buy (rather than lease) the list. That way, you can use it over and over again. The rates will vary substantially from publication to publication. However, with a little research work, you may be able to take advantage of a very "hot" list at little cost.

Many small businesses, interested in reaching only a select group of prospects in a specific geographic area, will obtain highly targeted lists. For instance, a plumbing supply store might ask for a list of new home owners and building contractors in a certain zip code area.

Another good idea along these lines is to stage a promotion that requires a person's business card as the "entry blank." You see this technique quite a bit at trade shows; it's also used occasionally by restaurants trying to target repeat customers. Once you transfer the cards to your label system, the odds are that you'll have a list of above-average quality--though, of course, a great deal will depend on how you use the list. You should still expect a relatively low return rate with this method.

This may sound like one of those questions that can only be answered by a response that's illegal, immoral, or compromising. Nevertheless, even though it may seem suspiciously easy to do, you can obtain top-quality software for your marketing efforts--legitimately--at a net expense of zero dollars.

The answer to a budget-conscious computer user's dream is called "shareware." This is software developed by independent programmers, not huge corporations with many salaries to pay and high overhead costs. The "shareware" idea goes something like this: the programmer invests his own time in developing a piece of software for a certain application (a word processor, for instance); he distributes it either on his own or through various computer outlets, free of charge--but with a request for voluntary payment, usually less than $50, flashed every time the user logs on.

In addition, the opening menu of a "shareware" program usually features a request that the user pass along a copy of the software to interested friends and associates. The result is something akin to an underground network of users, a percentage of which do in fact volunteer to pay the suggested fee. This allows the designer (in theory, at least) to realize some return on the time he's invested.

One of the first questions people ask about "shareware" is whether or not there are problems with the quality of the programs. The answer is, amazingly, no--if you pick the right developer and examine the package thoroughly before you commit to it. There are some programs available through the "shareware" network that are of very low quality indeed. But the nice thing is, they cost nothing to try, and you don't have to use them once you've obtained them! There's no risk whatsoever in examining any of the thousands of "shareware" programs available. And, more often than you'd expect, the software you come across is as good as--or even better than--the expensive commercial software.

Not all applications are available in "shareware" formats, but the most essential (database managers, word processors, and spreadsheets) are represented in abundance. Ask your computer dealer about information on how to obtain "shareware" programs.

One of the very best "shareware" lines is called ButtonWare. The main ButtonWare programs (PC-FILE, PC-TYPE, and PC-CALC) are all of outstanding quality, and more than hold their own against their higher-priced counterparts. It bears repeating that these excellent programs are available on a voluntary payment basis; however, if you eventually find ButtonWare's programs to be useful (and thousands of users have), you should strongly consider registering with the company. The typical suggested fee for a ButtonWare program is only $25. That represents one-tenth or less of the going rates for comparable retail packages. The software is well worth its asking price. You can reach Jim Button, the proprietor, by writing to: ButtonWare, P.O. Box 5786, Bellevue WA 98006.

It's hard for a lot of small businesses to accept, but economical testing represents a huge opportunity (and time very well spent), even though it may not feel like you're really doing anything profitable.

When you're testing out a new idea (rather than attempting to sell it to everyone you meet) you can make dozens of terrible mistakes. . . harmlessly. If "A" is going to kill you in large doses, you can test just a tiny bit and remark nonchalantly, "Hey, you know what? I think this is poison!"

Conversely, if "B" will give you big profits, you can bite off a little bit of that, decide you like it and THEN decide to go after it in a big way. In neither case do you risk your business "life" (read: profitability).

What's the alternative? Total commitment to every idea that sounds interesting. As you might imagine, that's very dangerous. Why risk everything if you don't have to? Test them all out. It's done all the time by the major companies, who simply cannot afford to wing it when millions of the firm's dollars are at stake.

Isn't it strange that much smaller companies so often feel that they must risk everything they have? Is it any wonder that over 80% of all new ventures go broke in a few years?

How do you do it? Simple. Let's say you have five new ideas. (They might be about a brand new product or service, a public awareness campaign, or a fresh idea in packaging. In short, you can test anything you're about to spend money on.) Put each idea on a 3-by-5 card.

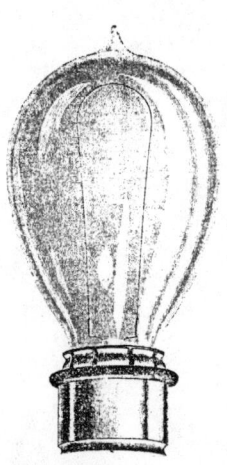

Now, find some "target group" members. Ask if they'd mind taking part in an informal survey. Obviously, the bigger the sample, the better. Ask your participants to rank the cards. The wording is important. Inform each subject that he or she is to put the cards in "the order that seems most important to you." (Do not alter this formula! It's proven quite effective.) Next, add up their answers. After tabulating the results, rank the ideas, one through five, based on the subjects' input.

The winner is probably your best bet. Don't fall in love with any one idea. What do you care which one makes you rich?

One important hint: always offer plenty of options. Never show someone just one idea and say, "Do you like this?" Your implication is that they'd better like it or you'll be heartbroken. Among the options, consider including your competition's product, service, ideas--or a cleverly-concealed approximation. How do you stack up?

Another winning (and time-tested) approach is the use test. Make up a few samples of your product). Give them away. Let people use whatever you give as they see fit--then, ask them to write down their reactions. Get them to tell you what they liked best. Why. How you can improve the item. You may even want to formalize your approach and supply each user with a questionnaire. Doing so is an inexpensive approach that can yield valuable results. Shoot for a minimum of a dozen such responses. One hundred or more is best.

You might even consider a small-scale market test. Go into a small town (or: use a small mailing list) (or: select a low-profile medium). Try to get set up a model by convincing a few stores to stock your item on a trial basis. See what happens and measure it carefully. Don't go to all this trouble and waste vital information by keeping inadequate records.

Keep such tests small (or, to use a quaint term I always find appealing, cheap). Keep an open mind. Make sure things stay manageable. There's no point in getting grey hair over a test, after all. You want to save that for the real thing.

Well-constructed tests save you headaches, ulcers, disasters . . . everything, in short, that small businesses have quite enough of already. Look before you leap!

ON THE HORIZON

How can you be sure you'll know what the economy is headed toward in coming years?

★

The following table can bring you up to date on current demographic "snapshots"-- and important developing trends. Big companies commission market research surveys and consumer studies that cost millions of dollars; that's probably out of your reach if you work in a smaller firm. But you will find the most significant outlines of the emerging economy of the 1990's summarized (briefly, of course) on the following pages.

A PORTRAIT OF AMERICA
Market Demographics for the Small Business
Fast Facts and Trends for the 1990s and Beyond

AGRICULTURE: Approximately 2.2 million farms. 2% of the population feeds 98% of the country.

BIG BUSINESS: Fortune 500 companies: most sell over $500 million annually. Fortune 1000 companies: most sell at least $100 million. Total U.S. corporations: about three million.

SMALL BUSINESS: Describes approximately 98% of all companies. 40% of the population would like to own a small business someday. Small businesses employ 4 out of every 10 workers. Nine out of ten new jobs are created by small businesses.

EMPLOYMENT: Total U.S. work force is approximately 120 million. About 5% of population is unemployed. Approximately 50% of all workers are women.

EDUCATION: Sixty million Americans are in a school of some sort. One-fifth of the population is estimated to be college grads.

FOREIGN TRADE DEFICIT: $141 billion.

HEALTH: Approximately 7,000 hospitals. Average U.S. life expectancy: 75 years.

HOUSING UNITS: 88 million. New construction: approximately 1.8 million per year. Average price of a new home: $150,000.

INCOME: Up 2%-3% per year. Average per capita income: $17,000. Median farm income: $30,000. Poverty line: $10,000. (Seven million fit this definition.) Social Security recipients: approximately 38 million. Inflation: ranges, but usually between 2-4% per year.

MAIL: Average addressee receives 611 pieces per year.

MOTOR VEHICLES: 177 million cars on the road. Eight million purchase new cars every year. Motor vehicle deaths: 48,000 per year.

NEWSPAPERS: Approximately 2000 dailies.

POPULATION: Total estimated in 1990: 250 million. Under age 24: 90 million. Over age 65: 30 million; but gaining approximately two million per year. Births: 3.7 million per year. Deaths: 2.1 million per year. Population growth: up almost 1% per year. Rule of thumb for estimating any "age point" (i.e., how many people are 24 years old in U.S.): ROUGHLY 3.5 million. "Baby boomers" (born 1945-1955) now in mid-thirties to mid-forties.

REGIONAL GROWTH: South is largest "sector" with 83 million residents.

URBAN VS. RURAL GROWTH: Estimated population living in "metropolitan areas": 184 million. Estimated population living in "non-metropolitan areas": 63 million.

COMPONENTS OF "SERVICE ECONOMY"

Communications
Education
Recreation
Retail
Repair
Finance
Government
Law
Utilities
Medicine
Transportation
Insurance
Cultural and Artistic
Religion

TEN MOST POPULOUS STATES

California (28 million)
New York (18 million)
Texas (17 million)
Florida (12 million)
Pennsylvania (12 million)
Illinois (12 million)
Ohio (11 million)
Michigan (9 million)
New Jersey (8 million)
North Carolina (6 million)

TEN LEAST POPULOUS STATES

Nevada (1 million+)
Idaho (998 K)
Rhode Island (986 K)
Montana (809 K)
South Dakota (709 K)
Delaware (644 K)
North Dakota (612 K)
Vermont (548 K)
Alaska (500 K)
Wyoming (490 K)

TEN TOP METRO MARKETS

New York (17 million)
Los Angeles (13 million)
Chicago (6 million)
San Francisco (6 million)
Philadelphia (6 million)
Atlanta (5 million)
Boston (4 million)
Dallas (4 million)
Houston (4 million)
Miami/West Palm Beach (4 million)

TEN ONE MILLION MARKETS

Buffalo NY
Chattanooga TN
Cincinnati OH
Columbus OH
Oklahoma City OK
Fresno CA
Greensboro NC
Greenville SC
Hartford CT
Jacksonville FL

... a Marketing Budget

TEN POPULAR TEST MARKETS

Appleton WI
Atlantic City NJ
Binghamton NY
Charleston WV
Columbus GA
Johnstown PA
Macon GA
Brownsville TX
Charlotte NC
Daytona Beach FL

GENERAL TRENDS

Older population (12% or 30 million 65 years or older).
People marrying later in life.
People having fewer children.
People having children later.
One-person homes: 21 million and growing.
Big "move-to" areas: South and West.
Big "move-away" areas: North and East.
Trendsetting state: California.
Hispanic population: 20 million and growing.
Imports: on the rise.
Manufacturing: more foreign-owned.
Gross national product: up 3% a year.
Service industries now account for 66% of jobs.
Major emphasis on quality control.
Women soon to be majority of managers.
Population growth in U.S.: near zero.
Population, world: soon to be 5 billion.
China: one fifth of world population.
Education: stronger emphasis.

Employment: people-oriented; service; information.
Workforce: more retraining for new positions.
Unions: fewer; more responsible.
Automation: increased emphasis.
Fewer manufacturing firms in U.S.

LIFESTYLE TRENDS

TOP RECREATION: TV.
SAVINGS: Averages 7% of pay.
PETS: 50 million dogs; 55 million cats.
SMOKERS: 33% of population.
DIETERS: 33% of population.
EXERCISERS: 20% of population.

Instantly Organize Your Entire Business

Save time and money every day!
Over 200 forms ready-to-copy and go to work for your business.

Our popular book, *Ten-Second Business Forms*, will help organize your business, professionalize your image, and save you time and money every day.

With this book and a standard office copier, you can save countless hours -- and thousands of dollars in printing costs -- by photocopying the essential graphs, charts, memos, invoices, and accounting records that most businesses buy or have produced by expensive outside printers.

Paperwork is crucial to every business. Whether you're collecting overdue accounts, setting an agenda, keeping tabs on your inventory, writing a sales report, or simply issuing any of the hundreds of documents, from purchase orders to receipts, that your firm must utilize month after month -- the forms you use must be businesslike in appearance, clearly laid out, easy to understand, and (most important of all) economical. Ten-Second Business Forms provides hundreds of reusable forms for virtually every business application, in a convenient comb-binding format that makes copying fast and easy.

By photocopying a single batch of forms, and bypassing printing costs and delays, you can easily recoup the price of the book with its very first use -- and continue to save money every time a new form is copied.

Thorough organization and systematic record-keeping is a vital ingredient for building sales and profits for any business. *Ten-Second Business Forms* will organize your business immediately, save you time and money, and improve the image you project to your customers, suppliers and employers.

TEN-SECOND BUSINESS FORMS

Comb binding allows easy photo-copying

Save time and money every day!
Over 200 forms and charts ready-to-copy:
- Invoices
- Receipts
- Statements
- Schedules
- Overdue notices
- Purchase orders
- Time cards
- Expense reports
- Sales slips
- Car logs
- Graphs, grids
- Much more...

Robert L. Adams, MBA, Harvard Business School

Paperback; convenient comb binding;
9" x 12"; $12.95

**ORDER TOLL FREE
1-800-872-5627**

Or send $12.95 + $2.75
shipping and handling to: Bob Adams, Inc.
260 Center Street
Holbrook, MA 02343

COLD CALLING TECHNIQUES
(That Really Work!)

by Stephan Schiffman

You smoke a cigarette... wander by the water cooler ... glance at the clock on the wall... and realize that the time has come. You look at the phone, slowly lift the receiver, and face a salesperson's greatest dread: the cold call.

If you're a salesperson faced with the constant, bewildering problem of "getting those appointments," you know how difficult it can be to turn a list of names and phone numbers into a calendar filled with solid prospects waiting to meet you. It can be done, and COLD CALLING TECHNIQUES offers a comprehensive and proven six-week plan that can make the cold call an opportunity, not a chore, for novice and veteran alike.

By following the plan that's worked for thousands of salespeople at top companies, you will:

- Discover the one simple phrase that can turn around the vast majority of all objections
- Learn how to be your own sales manager
- Find out how to monitor your calls and set goals based on your personal statistics
- Determine exactly how much time per week you should allot to cold calling
- See how business is like war - and what exactly your role is on the battlefield.

COLD CALLING TECHNIQUES (That Really Work!) will change a salesperson's attitude about the cold call, about personal goals, about sales as a profession, and will show the way for every salesperson to make a lot more money. Take the challenge to become more effective on the phone, more productive in your schedule, and more likely to land sales.

Stephan Shiffman is President of D.E.I. Management Group, Inc., a sales training firm. He has successfully trained nearly 200,000 salespeople for such companies as AT&T, Honeywell, and Prudential-Bache.

Paperback, 6" x 9" • $6.95

ORDER TOLL FREE
1-800-872-5627
In MA: (617) 767-8100

Or send $6.95 + $2.75
shipping and handling to:

Bob Adams, Inc.
260 Center Street
Holbrook, MA 02343